# Building the Gannett/USA TODAY Corporate Headquarters

William Pedersen for Kohn Pedersen Fox

First published in the United States of America by Edizioni Press, Inc.
469 West 21st Street New York, New York 10011
www.edizionipress.com

ISBN: 1-931536-10-4

Library of Congress Catalogue Card Number: 2002090587

Printed in Italy

Design: William van Roden
Editor: Sarah Palmer
Editorial Assistants: Jamie Schwartz, Aaron Seward

Cover photo: Timothy Hursley
Back cover sketch: William Pedersen

# A New Machi

# ne in the Garden

by Joseph Giovannini

William Pedersen's sketches demonstrate a variety of two-building schemes that eventually led to the final scheme.

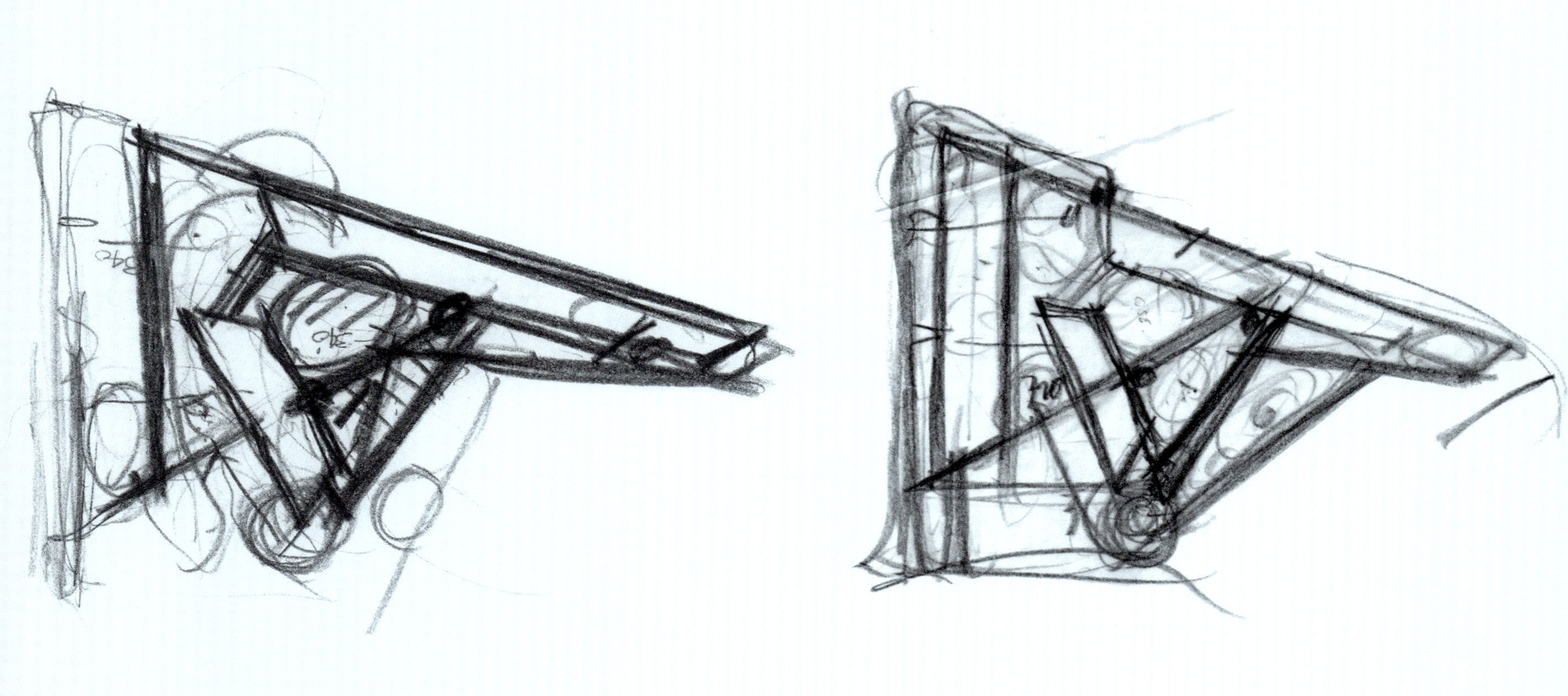

Depending on the angle of the sun and your viewpoint, the long vertical glass fins projecting from the façades of the Gannett/USA TODAY Headquarters in McLean, Virginia, haze the curtainwalls, creating a glowing green halo. Sometimes the glass fins literally sparkle; other times they emit rainbows at their edges. At a distance, the thin panels create what seems to be an aura around a building whose expanses of glass shimmer in a semi-transparency that recalls Oz, the Emerald City. Compared to the other solid and stocky buildings in Tysons Corner, Kohn Pedersen Fox's design looks spectral, a vision caught in a flux oscillating between the material and immaterial. Up close, the façades are mirage walls: when your eye reaches out to find an edge, the filmy surfaces seem to recede, farther than you think, not quite there, into indeterminate depth.

Tysons Corner may be a thriving regional center that has, by spontaneous generation, established a pattern of growth for edge cities, but for most city planners, the development lives in infamy as the placeless by-product of off-ramps, where cars park in an alienating ex-urban anomie. There is an illusion of nature here, or at least an allusion to it, because the parking lots that surround the office buildings are fringed with trees and bushes that collect in peripheral vision into the passing suggestion of a forest: Only on higher floors does the benign, comforting screen of trees give way to the visual fact that Tysons Corner is carpeted in parking, property line to property line. The trees no longer really constitute a forest any more than the buildings a city. People drive to the parking lot and step from one bubble into another, an elevator, which negotiates floors within the largest bubble, the self-contained building. The pancake organization itself isolates people from each other. Even the climatic containerization seals people off from the outside, creating an antiseptic relationship to the surrounding grounds. The environment is successively antisocial.

Over the last architectural generation, "context" has driven the logic behind many designs, and the prevailing paradigm in Tysons Corner—a point building or office block surrounded by landscaped parking—originally set up the assumption that KPF, one of the country's preeminent designers of corporate towers, would follow the established example. For the new 800,000-square-foot headquarters, a tower was the apparent solution, probably sited on the highest ground of the trapezoidal site.

An analysis of the land and program, however, soon convinced the architects to pursue another path. Building at the top of the site, with its stand of mature trees, would have compromised its best qualities, since the building's floor plate, not to mention the parking, would have erased the trees and dominated the rise. Migrating the building from the high, narrow end of the wedge to the low, wide end allowed the architects to consider other morphologies that did not require height and the strict pancake organization of an extruded tower. Simultaneously, the program itself militated in favor of another typology. Two organizations make up the company—USA TODAY and Gannett Co., Inc.—and each required news floors. Newspapers are highly social organizations necessitating frequent face-to-face interaction in groups and spontaneous one-on-one encounters. Roomy, undivided floor plates facilitate communication better than stacked floors broken up by opaque elevator cores. The availability of land and the prospect of contiguous rather than pancake news floors encouraged the plan to spread, and the bipolar program argued for a division of the building into separate but linked building masses.

What allowed the architects to think about dividing the building and growing the floor plate beyond the usual perimeters, however, was the willingness of Gannett to pay for a parking structure. Two thousand parking spaces were required for approximately 1,800 employees, each of whom has a car, and guests. That many cars parked on a surface lot, even on 25 acres, would have severely limited architectural possibilities. With a parking structure, however, the designers could containerize the parking rather than the people, and free much of the site for an expansive park.

Once the program was liberated from the constraints of a point tower and attendant parking lots, the architects could respond to the dynamics of the site and program so that the building would grow organically rather than conform to the formula of a box.

Early sketches of the two-building scheme, on the hilltop site.

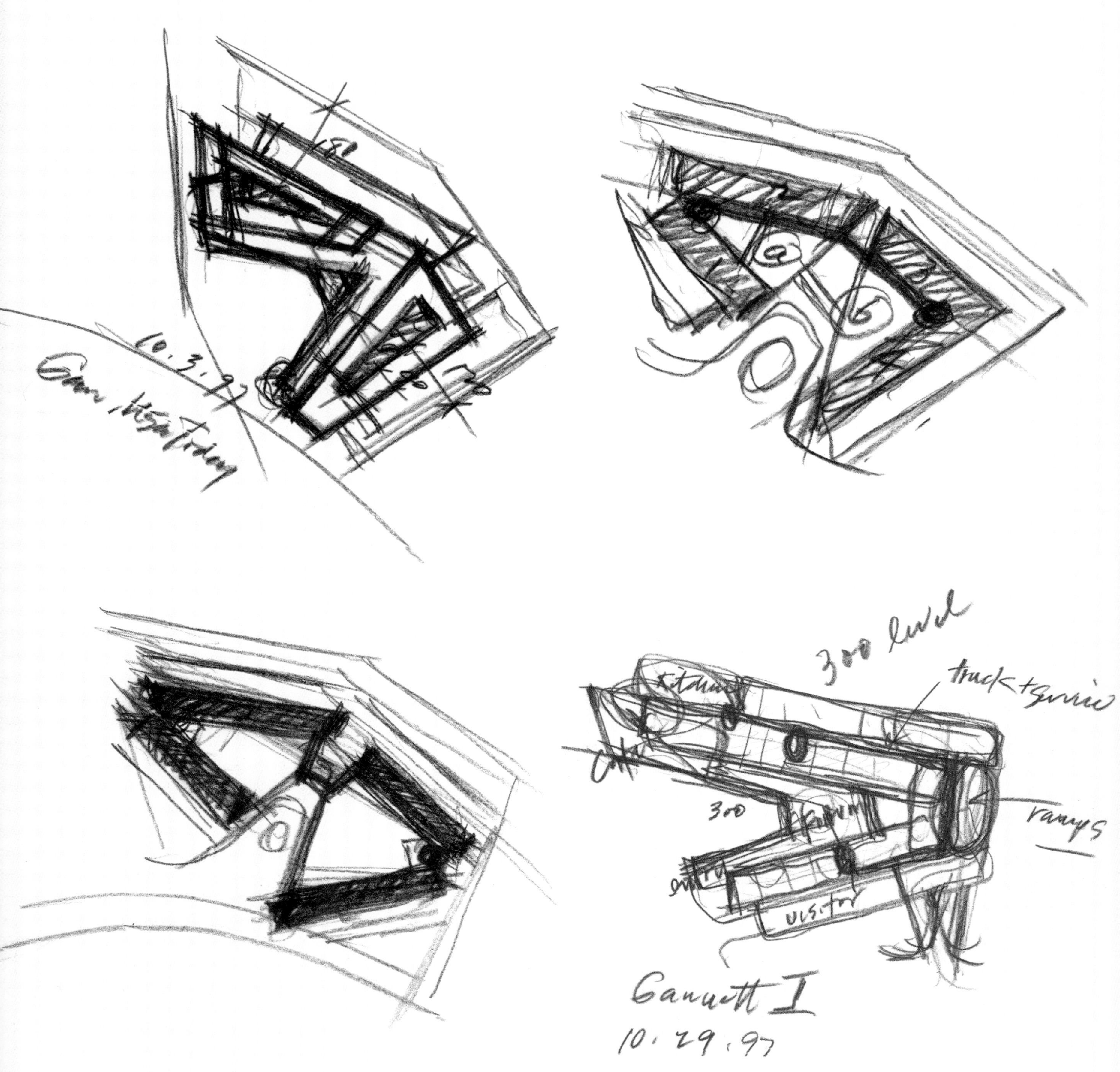

Sites usually have more contexts than just the architectural style of the buildings next door, and for KPF, the dominant consideration was the angled trajectory of the Dulles Toll Road along the northeast boundary of the property: the highway encouraged the architects to use part of the building strategically, as a sound barrier, to protect the site. A parking structure placed at the northwest edge would also protect the site visually from a nearby existing building, crudely designed with aggressive geometric forms.

Inside, the need for two newsrooms fought against the geometry of a single building, or even a simple pair of buildings, and pushed the usually square, vertically organized envelope toward the concept of two complex spaces hyphenated together in a horizontal flow. Organizationally, the newsrooms gravitated to the lower floors, acting as podia for offices above. Common facilities such as the library and auditorium wanted to be located in the hyphenating link, and the public rooms, like the cafeteria, gym, and lobby, found their way to the ground floor near the trails, terraces, and pond, to relate directly to the outdoors. Once the individual components such as newsrooms, entry, parking, and offices escaped the totalizing logic of towers, blocks, and cores, the program broke into parts that could be expressed as independent volumes, stacked and layered. The elevators, too, were free to migrate from the geometric center elsewhere to places in apposition to the main spaces. What emerged was a nine-story structure housing USA TODAY's newsrooms and offices, and a 12-story structure for Gannett.

Forces from outside and within, then, started shaping a building diagram that was no longer geometrically rigid and contained, but increasingly plastic and free. With two connected wings, the parti took the shape of a U whose extremities would extend toward the site, embracing an outdoor space. An architectural language of relaxed, angular geometries evolved that was conducive to opening the building to the landscape in a reciprocal relationship.

The wedge-shaped property encouraged a trapezoidal parking structure and office wing whose northeast edge paralleled the highway. Because the USA TODAY newsroom floors needed more square footage, its wing grew longer than the opposite Gannett wing, and it reached toward a landscape that turned back to the shorter wing in an interlocking gesture. KPF's Design Principal, William Pedersen, allowed the form of the building to open in a modified U, one arm longer than the other, but with both ends tapered at an angle that avoids the confrontational geometry of frontal façades. By twisting the two wings out of symmetry, the architects prevented the self-containment of a traditional building, and opened the diagram to the site. The consequent parallelograms and rhomboids dynamize both the building and landscape. Eccentric rather than Euclidean, the basic parti escapes rigidity. The large structure keeps from becoming monumental; this is not a building whose verticality and mass stakes its claim to land, but a building that slips through the landscape with a subtlety that belies its size.

What motorists confront as they reach the crest of the hill on the Dulles Toll Road heading into McLean is not a massive block or tower but an agglomeration of horizontal and vertical masses that seem to grow out of each other in a prismatic organicism. Most remarkable is that the architects have dematerialized the masses, turning opaque solids into semi-transparent crystals. Seen from a distance, the 800,000-square-foot structure is a glaciated beauty with the strangeness of an apparition. Changing effects of light animate the icy green glass and hard-edged forms. The filmy surfaces seem slightly out of focus, yet they accurately reflect the clouds and sky. Surface dissolves mass.

A long, ceremonial drive leads visitors into a site that has been landscaped as a bucolic activity park, centered on a large storm water management pond, with a dam spilling water. A viewing pavilion hovers over the lower level. Paths for jogging and walking lace the area around the water, leading up to the high point of the site, where a baseball diamond is set among the mature trees.

The entrance drive leads to a complex of buildings that angles around a grassed courtyard crossed by a series of weirs running past shifted fieldstone walls, spilling down to the dam at the bottom of the rise.

From left to right, top to bottom, these models demonstrate the process behind the design's evolution. The high-rise on the hilltop, the original assumption for the project, is at top left. Top line: Multiple schemes are tested, compared, and contrasted. Second line: Schemes are refined or combined and evaluated. Third line: The breakthrough scheme moved the two individual components from the hilltop knoll to the new meadow site. This comparative design process is significant to Bill Pedersen's work, and is one he has used since designing his first project 35 years ago.

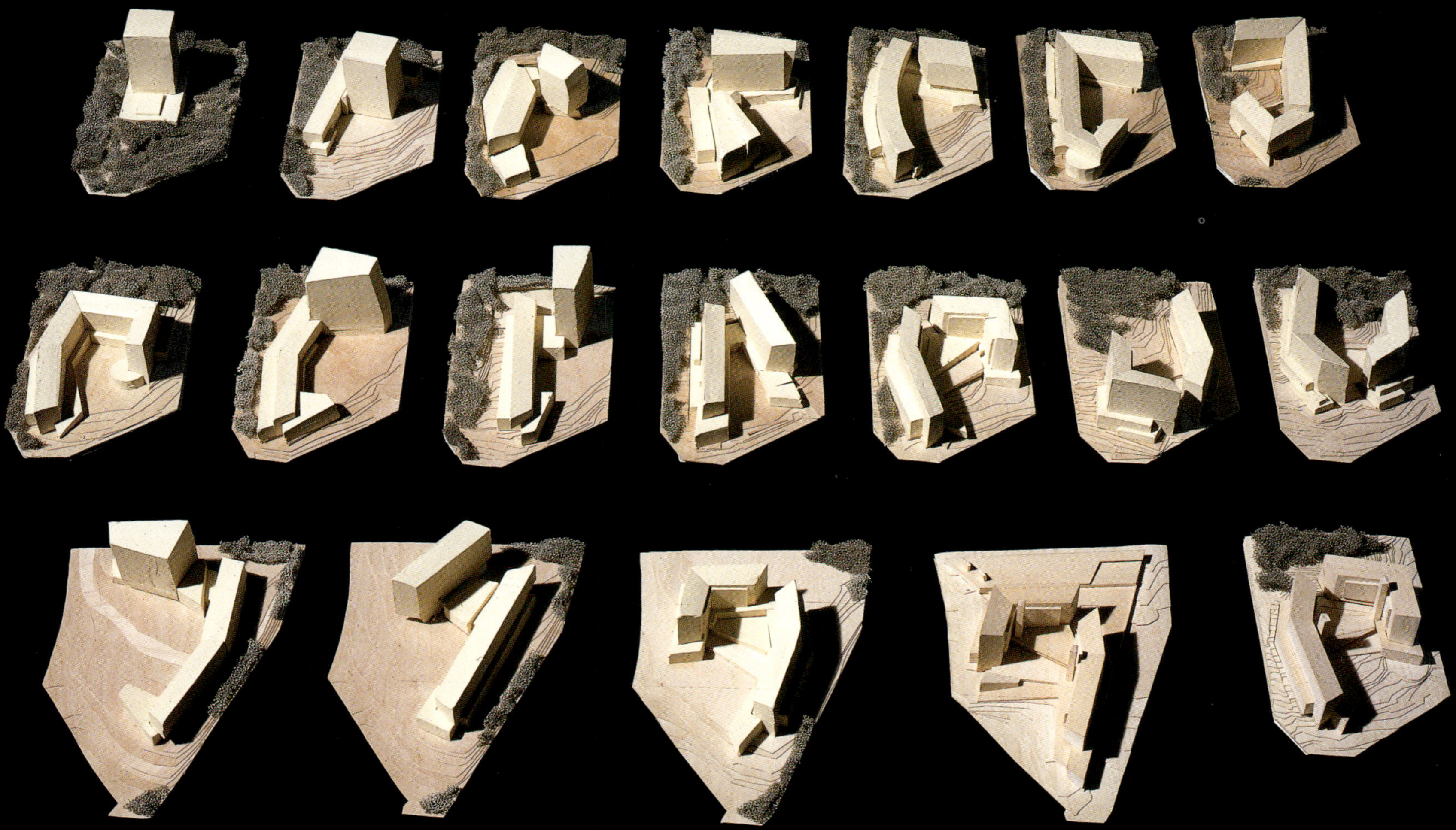

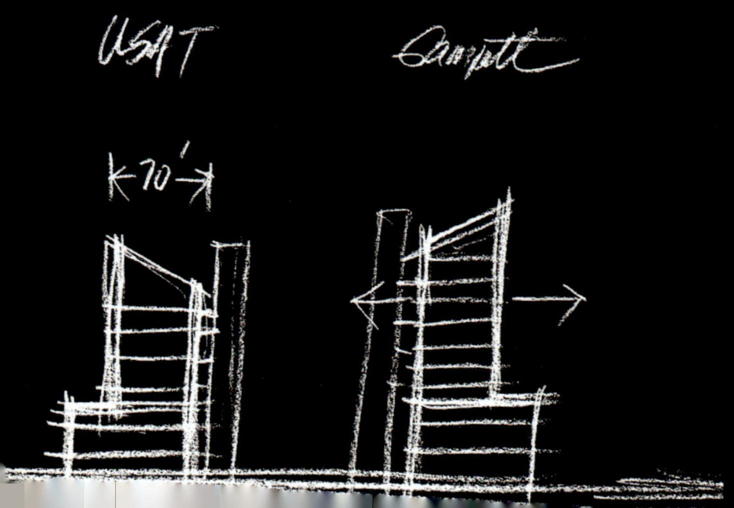

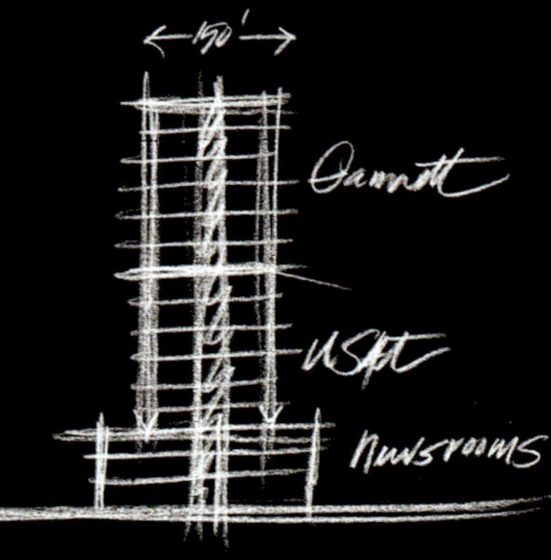


The left sketch shows the program that was used, comprising two smaller towers, connected by a low podium. Dimensionally, the idea of separate structures connected by shared functions was less conventional than an office tower, the early scheme shown at right.

Asymmetrically slung on one side of the prow-shaped edge of the Gannett wing, the brushed stainless steel entrance canopy opens into a long, vast two-story lobby sized to accommodate functions for 400 or more people. A stainless steel "harp" staircase, adjacent to a plate glass wall looking onto the courtyard lawn, rises out of a pool of Black Absolute granite set in a field of White Cherokee marble. The folded ceiling plane, leafed in aluminum squares, shimmers.

The space is a resultant of desire lines crossing front to back. At the far end of this impressive hall, corridors between the Gannett and USA TODAY wings intersect at the guard's desk, which also controls an axis leading from the parking structure. A random pattern marble, the individual pieces cut at angles contrary to the veins, carpets the path to the cars. It is here at the nexus of the building that the architects display their full material palette, introducing marbles, woods, metals, and glasses.

Besides summarizing the building's materials, the lobby introduces Gannett's wide spatial range. As in many parts of the headquarters, the harp stair constitutes a foreground piece with a strong visual identity. There are several such "moments," including a bridge between the wings, the dramatically raked ceiling of the boardroom, and the prows that terminate several volumes. The objects all mark space and help create a sense of place in what might be called the immediate, or near, distance.

Buildings that are not self-contained objects but environments sending wings out into their sites often offer sections viewable to each other, and the two Gannett wings facing each other occupy a middle distance. Circumferential plate glass windows on the lower floors offer deep axial views beyond, to the pond and to the wooded baseball diamond at the far end of the site. On the upper floors, views skim over the canopy of trees in the surrounding forest.

This is a building with both a here and a there, and the structure itself becomes an optical instrument that not only frames the views but establishes distances, near, middle, and far. You see with and through it, like a pair of binoculars. The building does not set itself apart from the view like a stand-alone object because it is part of the landscape. Gannett occupies the south wing, and USA TODAY the north, but the upper floors are not simply extruded up from the lower stories, which have a wider footprint that accommodates such common functions as the cafeteria and gym. The side of the building surrounding the courtyard steps back, forming outdoor terraces adjacent to glass perimeter corridors that U around the wide lawn at the heart of the design. Since the Bauhaus, Modernists have traditionally expressed circulation in glassy stairwells, but Pedersen here socializes the building by creating a confluence of pathways that engenders a public sphere that is both horizontal and vertical. Smokers cluster outside on terraces as others use the outdoor and indoor corridors to circulate within and across the building. The break-out space outside the auditorium occupies an esplanade that doubles as an interior corridor crossing over from one wing to the other. When the audience takes a break from a meeting, it moves into a public corridor. The architects have used necessities such as hallways and lobbies to foster the equivalent of small-town life. People on the ground floor see people on opposite floors. The façades may be cool aesthetically, but they are also occupied and active, humanized by the people inside.

Circulation is organized to foster encounters within larger social spaces that create a collective sense of community. Life in mid-rise and high-rise structures has long been suppressed by stratification and containerization; the KPF architects brought the activity to the surface and let it play, inside and out. The morphology of this terraced, U-shaped building pools people and gardens a sense of community. Terraced hillsides of Italian villages come to mind, where the life of the town is visible on the climbing paths. But Positano merges here with San Gimignano: the two glass towers, sheathed in textured, fritted, and transparent glass, house glass elevators that afford views onto the terraces, and vice versa.

This aerial photo shows the building, site, and surrounding area, heavy in highways and typically suburban.

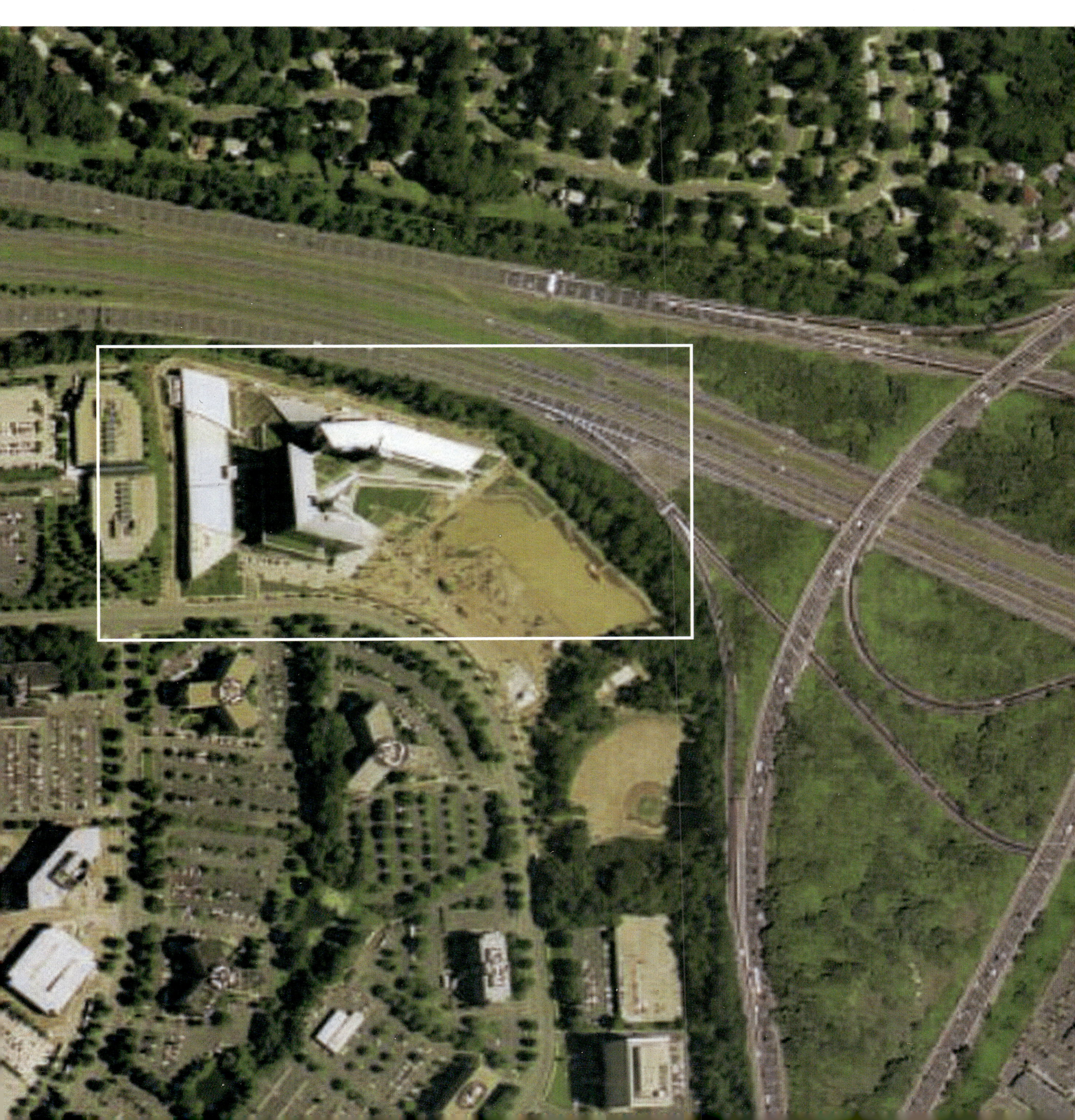

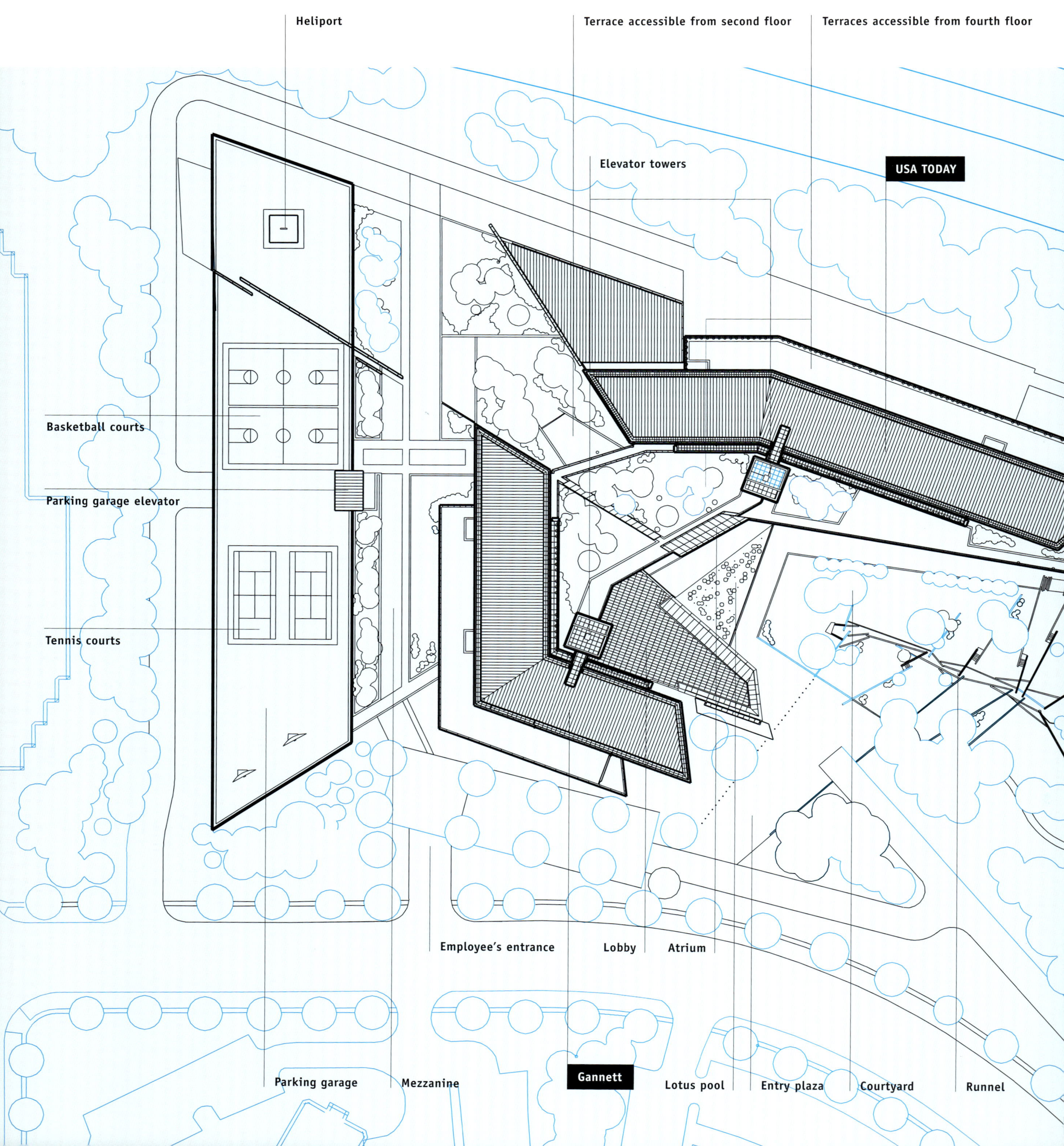

Heliport
Terrace accessible from second floor
Terraces accessible from fourth floor
Elevator towers
USA TODAY
Basketball courts
Parking garage elevator
Tennis courts
Employee's entrance
Lobby
Atrium
Parking garage
Mezzanine
Gannett
Lotus pool
Entry plaza
Courtyard
Runnel

Storm water managment pond
Pavilion atop overflow mechanism
North

Above: The pattern of logs floating down a river inspired landscape architect Michael Vergason in his design of the low fieldstone walls that terrace the graded hill. Below: Several ideas guided this particular construction. First, terraced topography accommodates the slope from the complex down to the storm water management pond. Second, Vergason wanted to shape the terraces in a way that tied the landscape into the building. The use of fieldstone in a sense reverses the walls that structure the base of the building volumes (see photo p. 93).

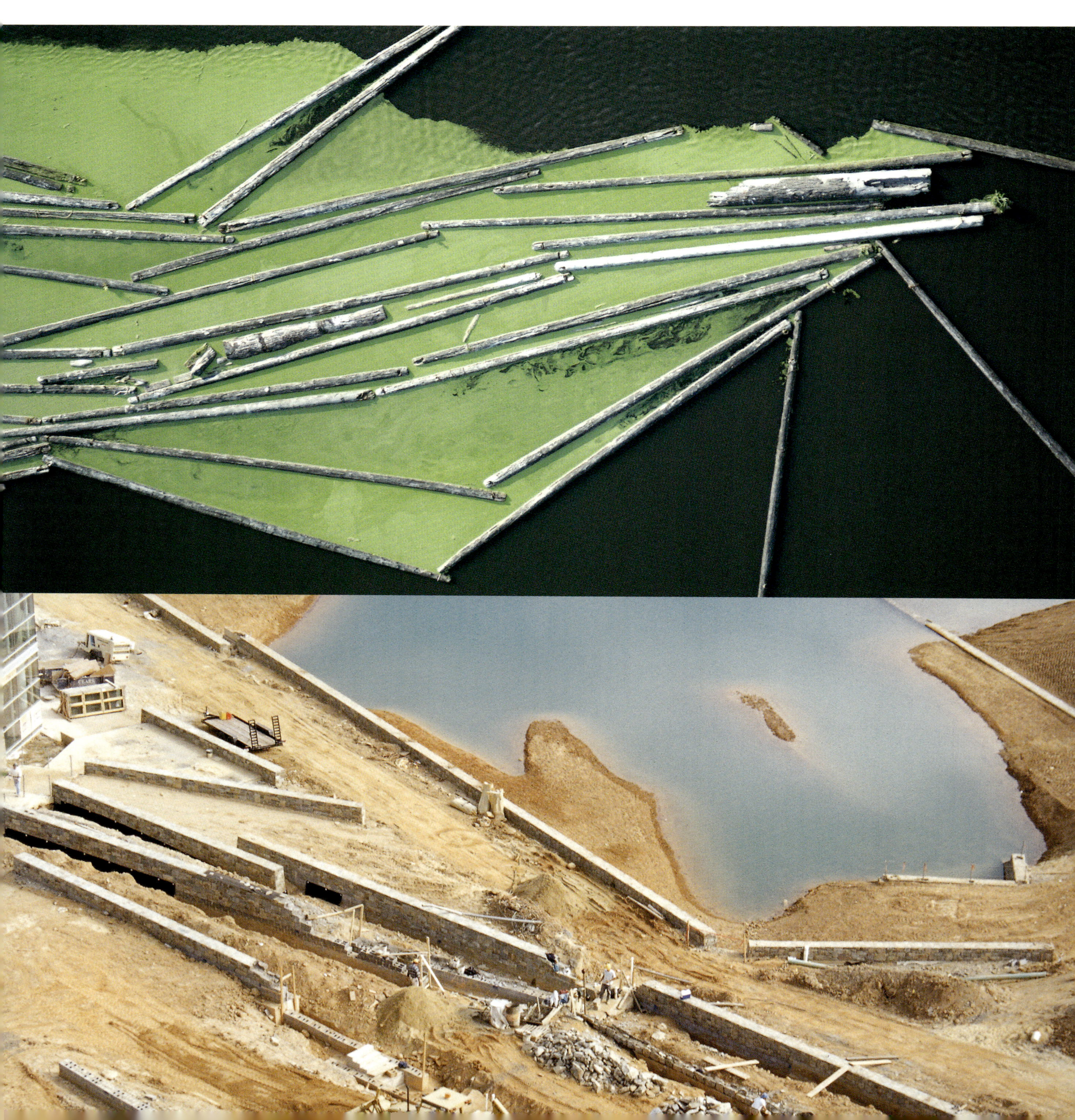

Tysons Corner represents a paradigm of ex-urban, freeway-dependent development, and the formal suggestion that Gannett's headquarters is a small, self-contained city is subversive in a context created by and for the car. The implication of most buildings at Tysons Corner is that you're either in the car or at the desk or moving efficiently between the two. The wisdom of KPF's Gannett is that the architects have elaborated the in-between space into a socializing public realm: you surrender your car at the garage to enter an environment that emphasizes pedestrian movement within a village-like plan that extends into the landscape. All levels of Gannett's corporate hierarchy, from CEO to mail clerk, walk these paths on what amounts to a democratic urban stage. Neither the landscape nor the building is passive to the other.

This façade of motion feeds, on the lower floors, newsrooms that are sweepingly open, pooling reporters and editors in spaces that support the sense of community. Producing a daily paper is a collective effort that requires an esprit de corps that architecture can help cultivate. By taking the elevators to the perimeter corridors, the architects open sight lines in the newsrooms, allowing editors and writers better visual access to one another. Without interruptive elevator cores, the architects encourage the flex space of today's more informal corporate cultures. Each newsroom also enjoys double views and natural light on two sides, a cross-illumination environmentally akin to cross-ventilation: the interiors seem informed by European office building standards about the proximity of occupants to natural light and views.

Connecting the two wings is a three-story structure that contains the library, theater, and other common spaces. The roof terraces atop this linking structure connect laterally to terraces and corridors along the adjacent two wings, creating a planted hillscape. But the stepped-back section invites the landscape onto roofs visible just outside the windows in shallow roof basins. Arlington-based landscape architect Michael Vergason plants simple, native materials in naturalistic flows—Buffalo grass, winterking hawthornes, iris. No trough is deeper than four feet (the soil increases the thermal mass of the building). Vergason extends the apparently chaotic geometries of the building into the landscape, a chaotically angled wall bordering the weirs. With open architectural forms flowing into the landscape, an environmental hybrid results that is unique in Tysons Corner, where you're either inside or outside a building. Horizontalizing the main masses helped Pedersen blur the building into Vergason's receptive landscape, part of an occupied continuum. The building belongs to the grounds from which it takes meaning. The clean, crisp lines of this machine in the garden underscores the rolling contours of the landscape.

The crystalline quality of the headquarters was not merely an aesthetic decision: it grew out of the need for natural light in the loft-like newsrooms. The views into the surrounding woods beyond the highway suggested glass curtainwalls, and once the architects determined that glass could handle the white freeway noise, they tried to soften the visual impact of an all-glass structure. KPF has always dimensionalized façades, often with reveals around windows. To add visual richness, the architects used fins to play one façade off another. Studies revealed that horizontal lines emphasized the spandrels while vertical bands brought out the mass of each volume. Because tightly spaced vertical metal fins looked like jail bars, the architects switched to glass. Laminated glass that could be exposed on edge had just become practicable. After profiling and sizing the fin, the architects developed a detail that allowed them to hide any suggestion of the mechanical connection holding it in place.

It is the vertical glass fins, spaced finally two-and-a-half feet apart, that initiates the effects of both indeterminacy and changeability in the façade. The fins generate a range of surface effects that transforms by the minute with the light. Collectively the fins vaporize the façades, removing the harshness of reflective glass and producing ephemeral effects. The sun, like a slide projector, casts the rainbows inside, often striating walls and floors in fugitive patterns of color that shift and vanish as the sun moves or dims: environmental phenomena activate a façade that has been set up to shift in unanticipated ways. The fins that dimensionalize the surface with a sense of shadowy depth and unpredictable light, then, also animate the interiors.

The runnel flows perpendicular to stepping fieldstone walls. Falls at each step aerate the water on its way to the storm water management pond, where silt settles and the water is further aerated and naturally purified for irrigation.

Collectively, the fins veil the façades, softening the overall geometries. But the architects deepen this effect of indeterminacy with their choice of glass: counterintuitively, this crisp, sharp, machine-crafted building loses both its commercial connotations and its sense of boundary and edge in the plays of reflection that result from mixtures of glass. The architects have deployed transparent, translucent, mirrored, textured, and fritted glass along with frosted mirrors throughout the building, launching a spontaneous array of visual side effects. Elevators riding up shafts of textured glass appear ghostly, and the translucent shafts themselves, reflected in adjacent façades, produce indeterminate views that are in turn faintly reflected by the shafts themselves. Looking out, occupants peer through veils that mystify views. The reflective green façade mirrors the sky, changing in color and opacity with the weather, season, and time of day. The architects glazed roofs bordering the courtyard, adding to the sense of transparency and fragility.

The fins, the choice of glass, and the spectral promiscuity reinforce the concept of indeterminacy that is based in Pedersen's use of elusive, non-Platonic shapes. The ice melts into the sky and landscape. Mysteriousness inheres in the prismatic building despite—or rather because of—the machine-made precision of the fins that can separate light into its constituent spectrum.

Beyond the catalogue of glass, the palette of materials is not only rich and beautifully orchestrated but chosen and detailed to materialize the basic concepts. The almost electrified patterns of the floor are randomly angled within skewed parallelogramatic shapes that emphasize overall conceptual forces. The graphically veined marbles in the lobby are patched in patterns that play with and against the stretched oblique geometries that shape the building masses. Rather than reinforcing the effect of solidity, the patterns craze the floors rhythmically. The Emerald Pearl granite surfacing the treads of the harp staircase suspends shiny flecks in what appears to be petrified water. The Black Absolute granite is even more depthless.

Besides dematerializing the ceiling of the entrance lobby with aluminum leaf, the architects used long-grain brushed stainless steel on the entry doors and in other metal components: the buttery color and lustrous sheen give life to forms struck by natural light. Even the façade of the garage is covered in perforated metal sheets that capture light, diminishing any sense of weight.

The architects warm the layered material collage with woods such as English sycamore and natural maple, pale and tending to abstraction. Although warm American cherry anchors walls in the more public rooms, the woods, like the rest of the materials, tend to dematerialize the buildings.

The Gannett headquarters represents a daring application of a vocabulary of sliding non-Platonic volumes that first appeared in Pedersen's work in the 1980s, in an experimental, break-out house in Vermont. Rather than importing idealized geometries to the hillside site, the architect allowed the views to spin the forms, resulting in an extroverted building that responded to the surrounding mountains, exposures, and topography. The design was contextually deferential, but the context was natural rather than architectural.

The house lost its orthogonality with the emergent diagonals, but the dynamic geometry did not imply speed so much as change. Diagonal lines, planes, and volumes seen against each other created the perception of continuous reconfiguration for the person walking through and around it, implying that the permanence of architecture had ceded to an experience of space that was phenomenal—a space of change. Pedersen used materials that would change over time, such as bronze, which acquires a greenish patina.

Pedersen brought these ideas into the corporate realm with his design for the IBM headquarters in Armonk, New York, in the mid-1990s. The strategy of angular geometries wheeling toward features in the wooded site proved equally valid at a larger scale, even with a much more complex program. The headquarters, intended for a leaner, more agile version of the company, replaced the previous headquarters designed by Skidmore Owings & Merrill nearby on the same site, a geometrically pure, right-angled structure that acknowledged nothing accidental or incidental. The shape of the new downsized headquarters reinforced more informal organizational needs in the new "flex" company. The CEO's office was located in an immutable power corner in the old building, with an exquisitely landscaped void in the center of the floor plate. In the new building, the CEO occupied a less symbolic position in a building that downplayed hierarchy. When Euclid gave way to nature, the new headquarters design relinquished its attitude as an inflexible and dominant object. In its pliancy, it acquired instead an ability to form a yin-yang relationship with the outdoors.

As viewed from the east, the project's various glass types respond to light in multiple ways.

The IBM building proved conceptually elusive since it could not be understood at a glance; like a Calder stabile, it offered instead configurations that evolved during a walk. The building provoked promenades, which implied duration. The angular geometries never merged into a single, comprehensible form but stayed divergent rather than convergent, multiple and independent rather than singular and fixed. The design departed from the juxtapositions of formally and materially disparate pieces of KPF's previous projects, in favor of a fragmented geometry whose forms broke and reconciled with each other almost organically. The materials remained varied, but within a limited palette that minimized the difference of the architectural parts and shapes. Predicated philosophically on change and self-transformation, the new IBM headquarters acknowledged architecturally what the information giant had painfully realized in the marketplace, that metamorphosis was the new cornerstone of a different world order.

The Vermont house has engendered many progeny among projects in the prolific KPF office, but the Gannett Headquarters represents one of the most completely developed iterations of a difficult idea at a large scale—nearly half the square footage of the Empire State Building. Rarely do ideas valid in houses translate to major projects, either formally or financially. The latent irony in the corporate commission is that the radical forms and detailing did not necessitate radically new construction techniques: construction was conventional, even with the many unique moments. Building the concept then did not cost an appreciable premium beyond the level anticipated for a headquarters of this stature. The icy aesthetic demanded precision, especially in an acutely angled curtainwall, and the architects took advantage of industrial production to economically manufacture parts that fitted together crisply. Principles of serial production applied to spaces and forms that were unique rather than universal. The high-tech harp staircase, suspended on stainless steel rods, for example, is anecdotal and unique rather than universal, like a Miesian staircase. Each construction element, whether the curtainwall, concrete floor plate, or steel skeleton, is a simple rather than complex construction system. They are only complex in their combination; they do not conform to a reductive geometry expressing a reductive concept. Standard building methods and materials are not used in standard ways.

Gannett, however, represents in its Darwinian evolution a step beyond its predecessors. Pedersen orchestrated many volumes into a complex collage in which the roof lines, which are sloped, shoot the eye into a perspectival play that seems to speed form. The building takes on a vectorial quality. The ideas were first posited at IBM, especially in interior spaces designed with forced perspective. At Gannett, Pedersen not only forces perspective, but multiplies it to work from many crossing viewpoints: the multiple perspectives accentuate the sense of depth because the perspectival illusions cross each other simultaneously, creating a relativistic spatial flux. The pedestrian becomes a moving eye in a decentered building where the perspectival lines do not add up to the rational whole of a classical Renaissance building. A pictorial irrationality infuses the glass prisms that house an otherwise rational interior: the building is not a one-liner, but a structure that eludes in its multiplicity easy understanding. The design is a paradigm removed from the typically rationalist structures in Tysons Corner that dominate their sites with self-confident, static Euclidean geometries that rarely flex. Inert in their fixed axialities and symmetries, they do not reconfigure themselves in the mind or eye through time.

The Gannett Headquarters is a conceptually and perceptually ambitious structure that succeeds in concretizing a philosophy of change. Rarely have architects addressed such a complex set of issues so convincingly and completely, pulling out all the stops, from concept and geometry, materials and details, to landscape, car, and community. They have successfully posited an alternative to the status quo of a point building in a parking lot. Gannett as a building is behavioral and participatory: it invites elements and people into an interactive environment that is set up to change. Occupants of this building walk through rainbows.

Planted terraces draw the landscape up and through the building, inviting outdoor activity. Movement in the elevator towers activates the courtyard space.

# Gannett Co., Headq

# Inc./USA TODAY uarters Complex

McLean, Virginia 2001

As seen from Jones Branch Drive, the distinction between sky and building is obscured by the reflective prism of the façade.

After multiple façade studies, the architects determined that the widespread use of glass would both lighten and unify the project.

The podium and landscaped terraces stitch together the two towers.

Massing, building orientation, and enhanced landscaping protect the central courtyard from neighboring highway noise.

Terraces, plazas, and courtyards at ground level and on rooftops allow work and dining on several levels, promoting a sense of shelter and security for the newspapers' around-the-clock activity.

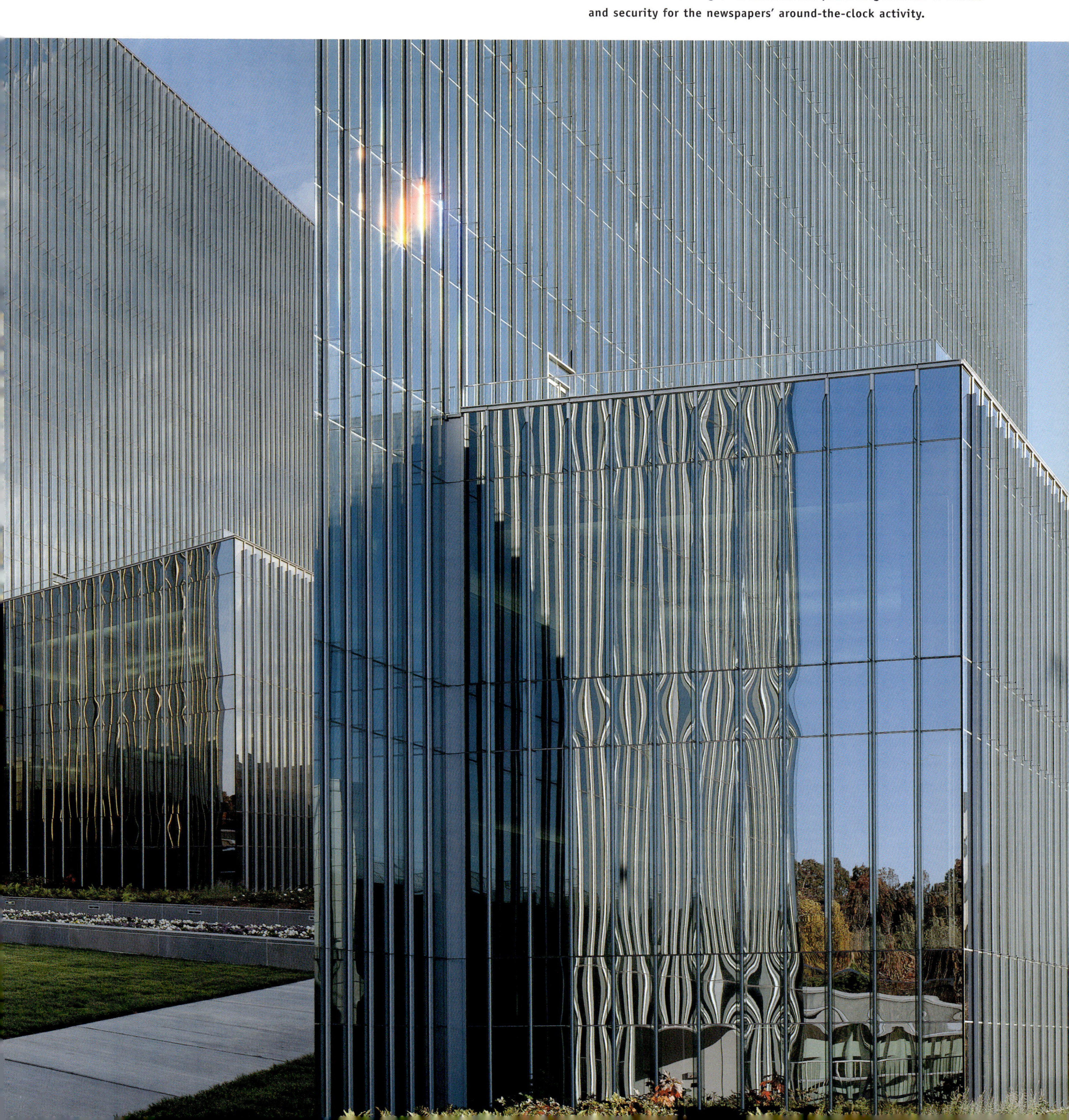

Relationship of building to earth.

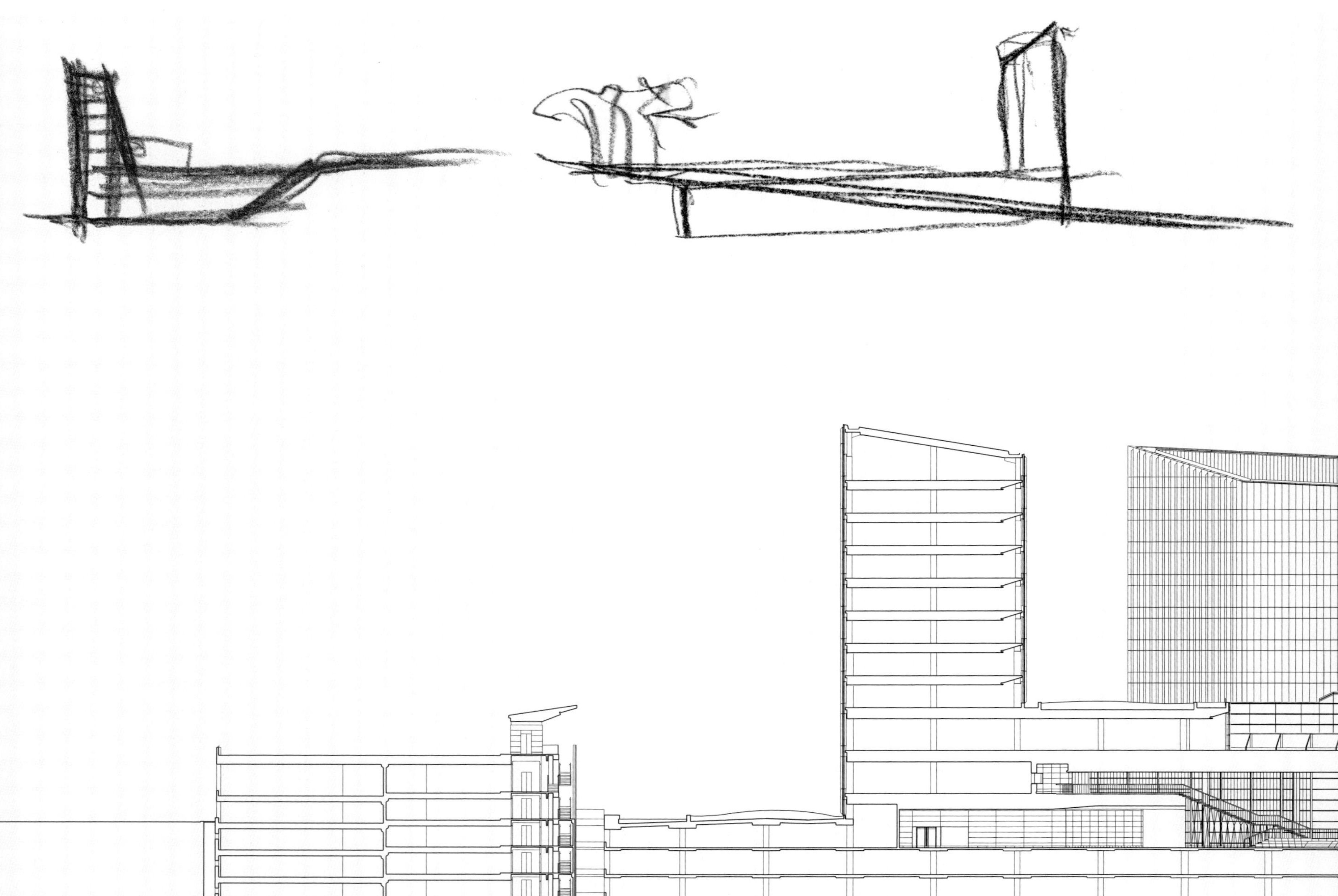

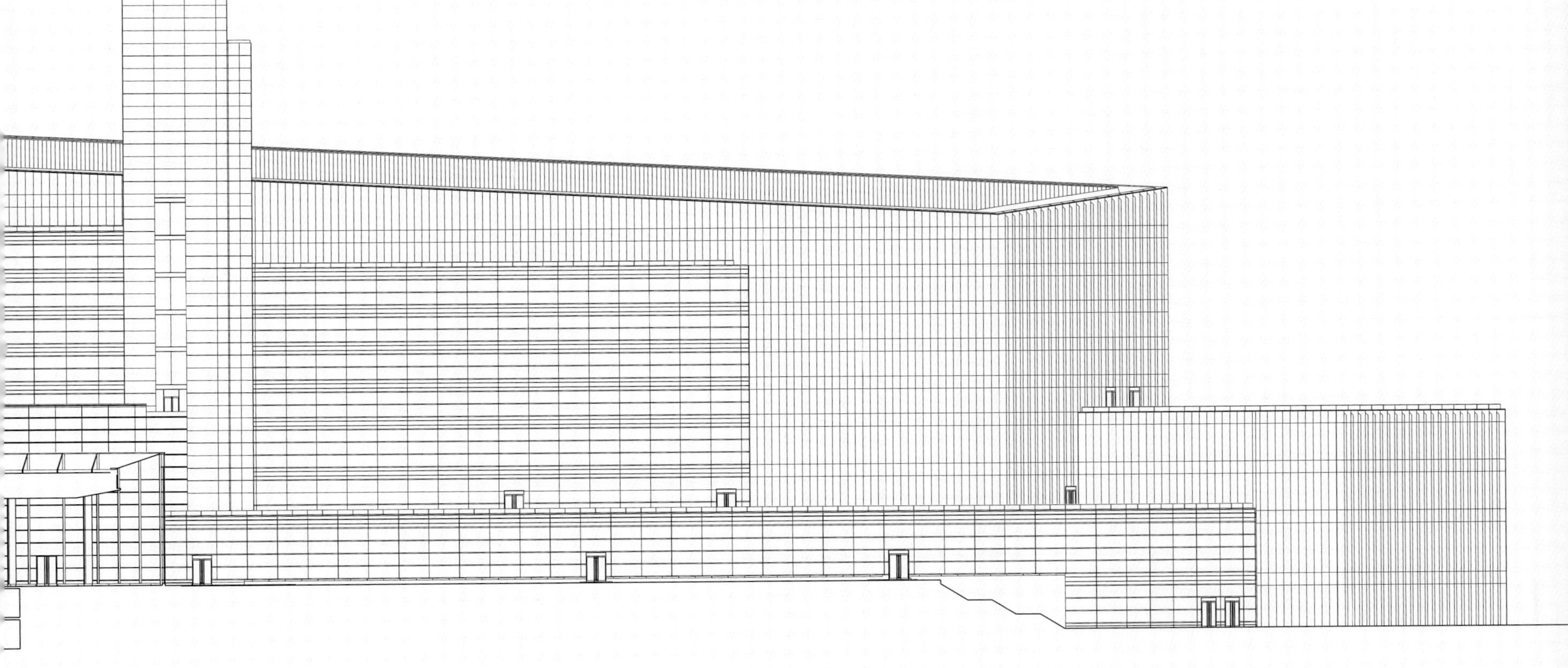

East-West section through parking, Gannett building, and lobby, showing the south elevation of USA TODAY building.

Sketch at left: section through Gannett and parking levels.
Sketch at right: spiraling forms of the two buildings.

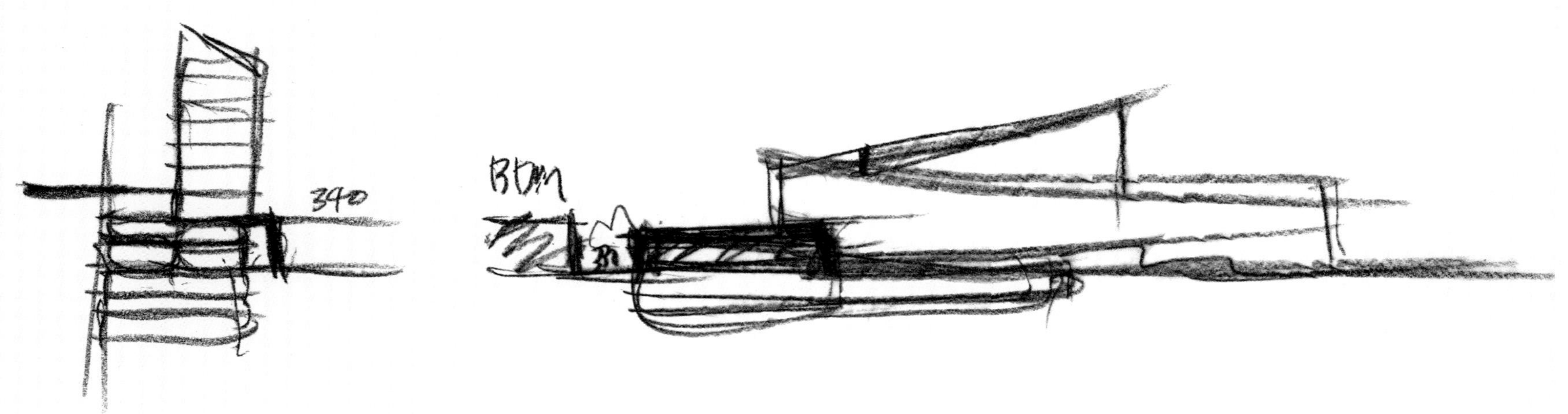

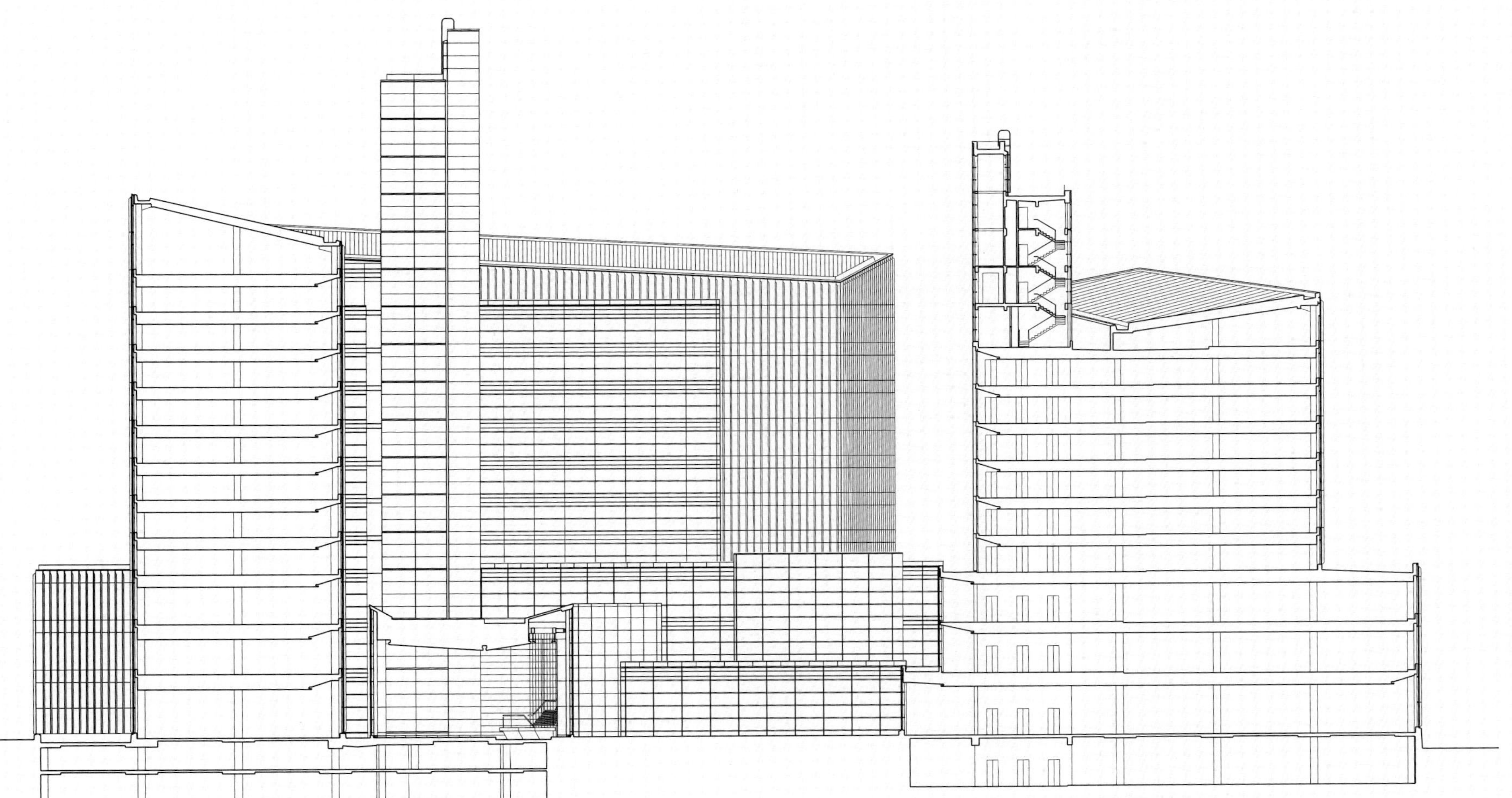

North-South section through Gannett (at left), and USA TODAY and its elevator tower (at right). Roof terraces are visible in the center.

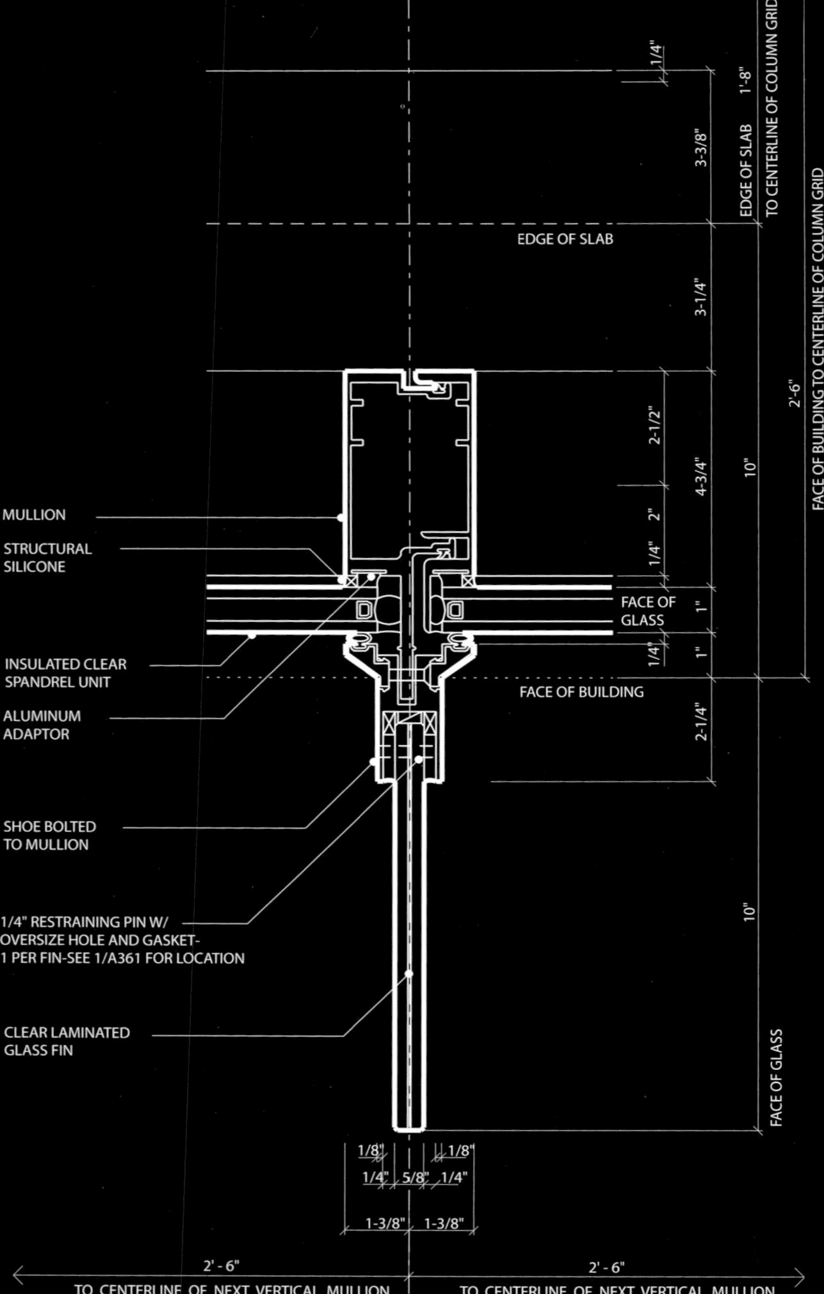
MULLION
STRUCTURAL SILICONE
INSULATED CLEAR SPANDREL UNIT
ALUMINUM ADAPTOR
SHOE BOLTED TO MULLION
1/4" RESTRAINING PIN W/ OVERSIZE HOLE AND GASKET- 1 PER FIN-SEE 1/A361 FOR LOCATION
CLEAR LAMINATED GLASS FIN
EDGE OF SLAB
FACE OF GLASS
FACE OF BUILDING
1/4"
1'-8"
EDGE OF SLAB TO CENTERLINE OF COLUMN GRID
3-3/8"
3-1/4"
2-1/2"
4-3/4"
2"
1/4"
1"
1/4"
1"
2-1/4"
10"
2'-6"
FACE OF BUILDING TO CENTERLINE OF COLUMN GRID
10"
FACE OF GLASS
1/8"
1/8"
1/4"
5/8"
1/4"
1-3/8"
1-3/8"
2' - 6"
TO CENTERLINE OF NEXT VERTICAL MULLION
2' - 6"
TO CENTERLINE OF NEXT VERTICAL MULLION

The understated angles of the towers' façades are covered in silvery reflective glass, interrupted at 30-inch modules by transparent vertical glass fins.

The projecting glass fins accentuate the angularity of the building.

From the paved entry plaza, the various glass forms
rise into the sky. Program elements are stacked, layered,
and articulated within the composition.

Clear glass marks circulation and public spaces.

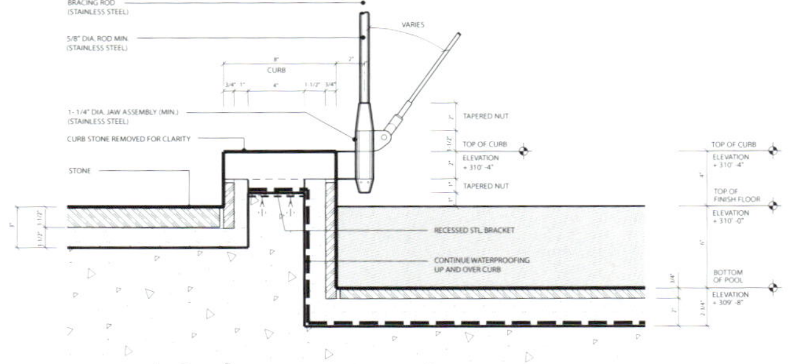


Circulation lines and activates the central space.

Lotus Pool

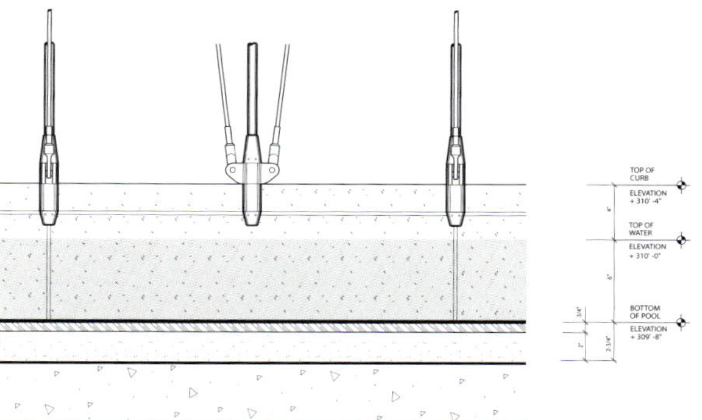


Fiber optic lighting in stainless steel wands creates a flickering plane above the water's surface.
Lotus plants and koi have yet to be introduced to the pool.

A back-lit billboard of the commissioned work by Ed Ruscha, *WORDS IN THEIR BEST ORDER*, marks circulation to the dining areas.

Glass volumes at various angles and transparencies form a layered composition.

Shared amenities are housed within the podium.

GANNETT
USA TODAY

Circulation is organized to foster encounters and make activity visible.

Surface parking is minimized to maximize green space.
The elevator core and an open set of stairs provide access to parking and rooftop activities. Light shafts bring daylight to the floors below.

Perforated aluminum panels on the above-grade portion of the parking garage provide a visual screen, shade, and lattice for climbing plants, as well as reduced nighttime light spill.

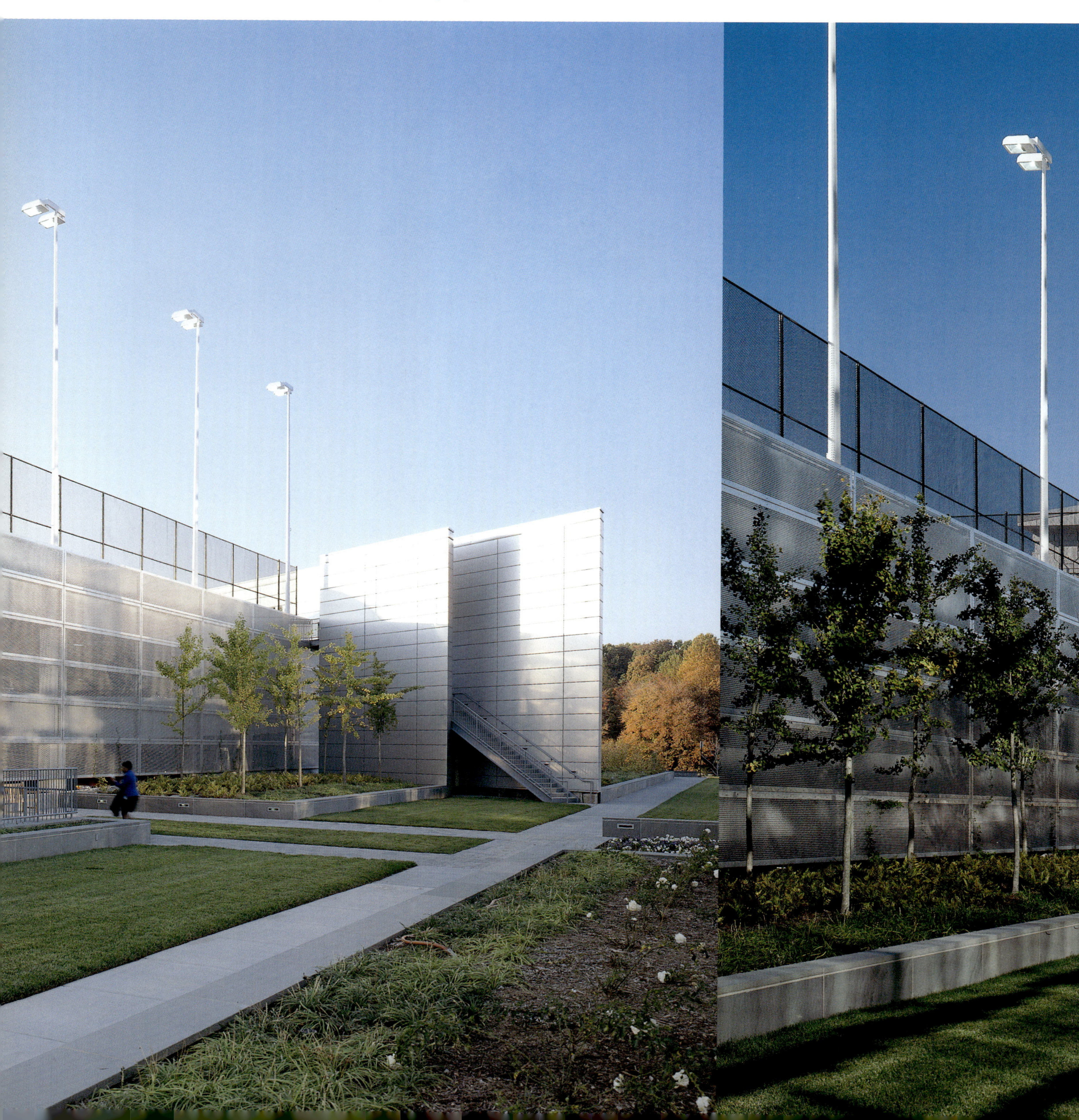

The roof of the parking garage is finished with basketball and tennis courts, a satellite and communications equipment farm, and a helipad.

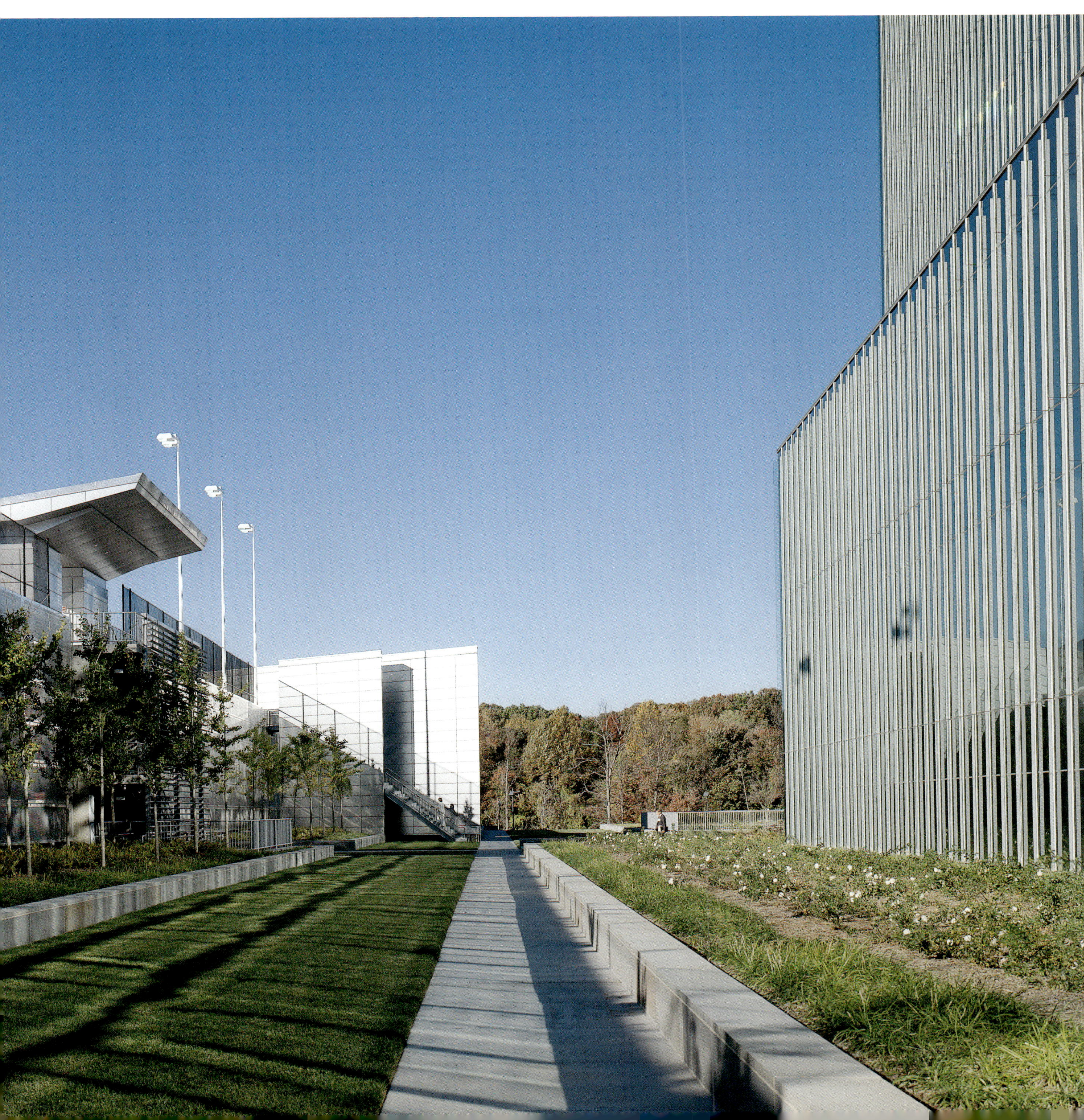

Two Landscape Schemes for Meadow Site

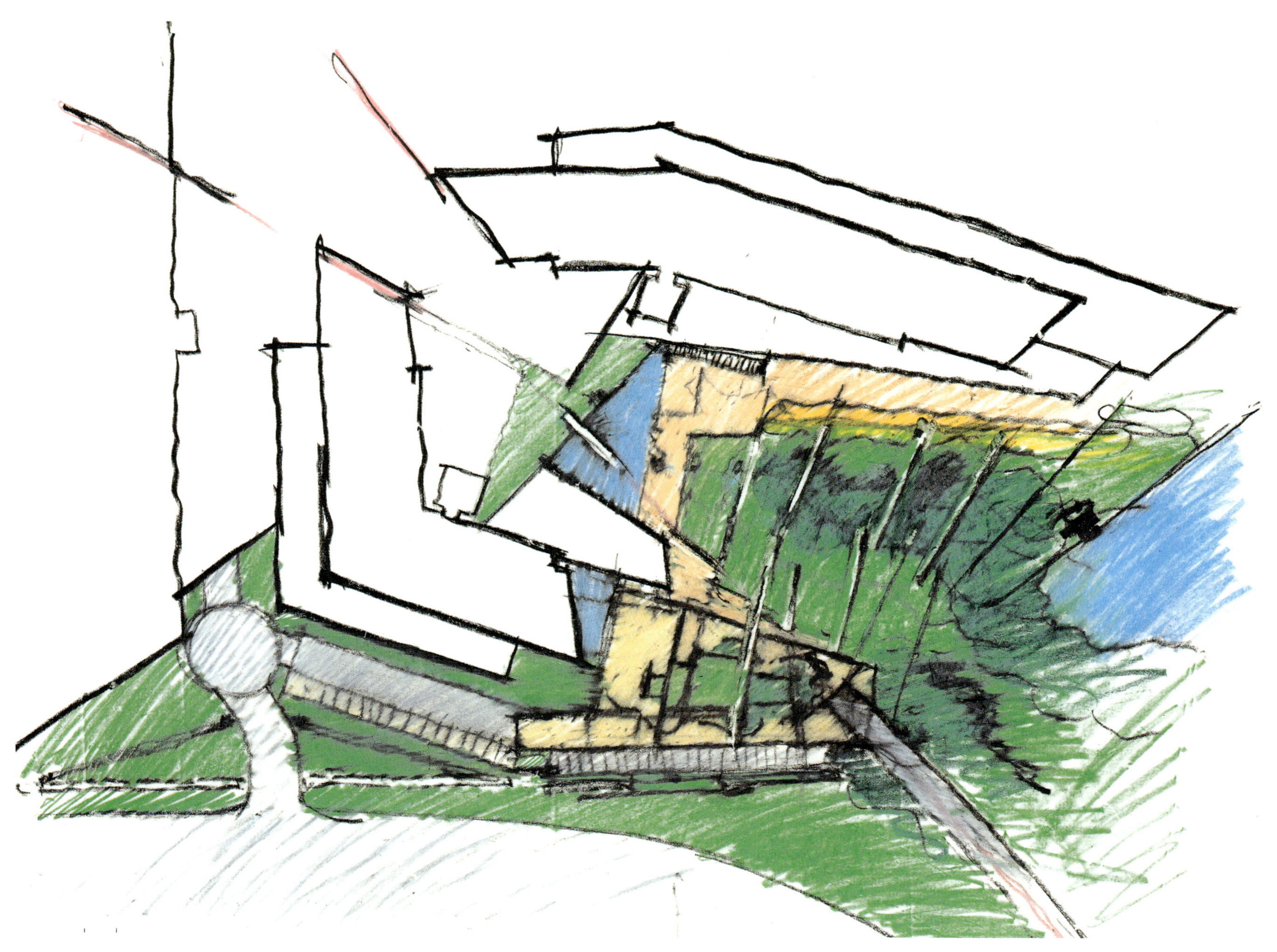

30 phy

## Terrace Landscape Development

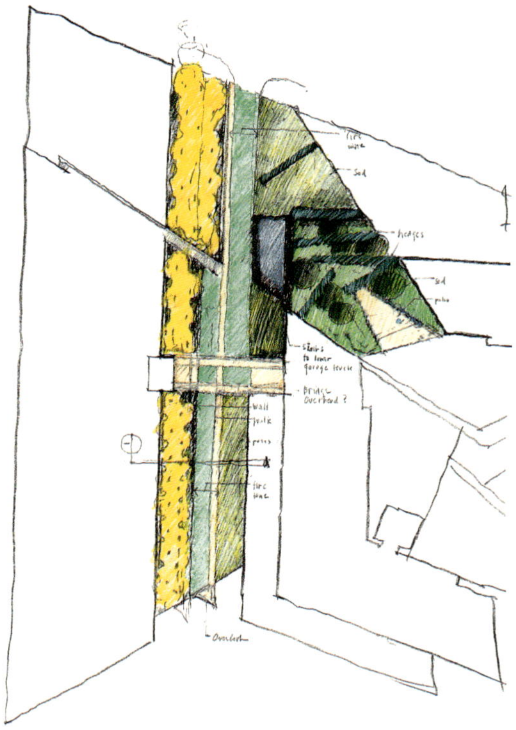

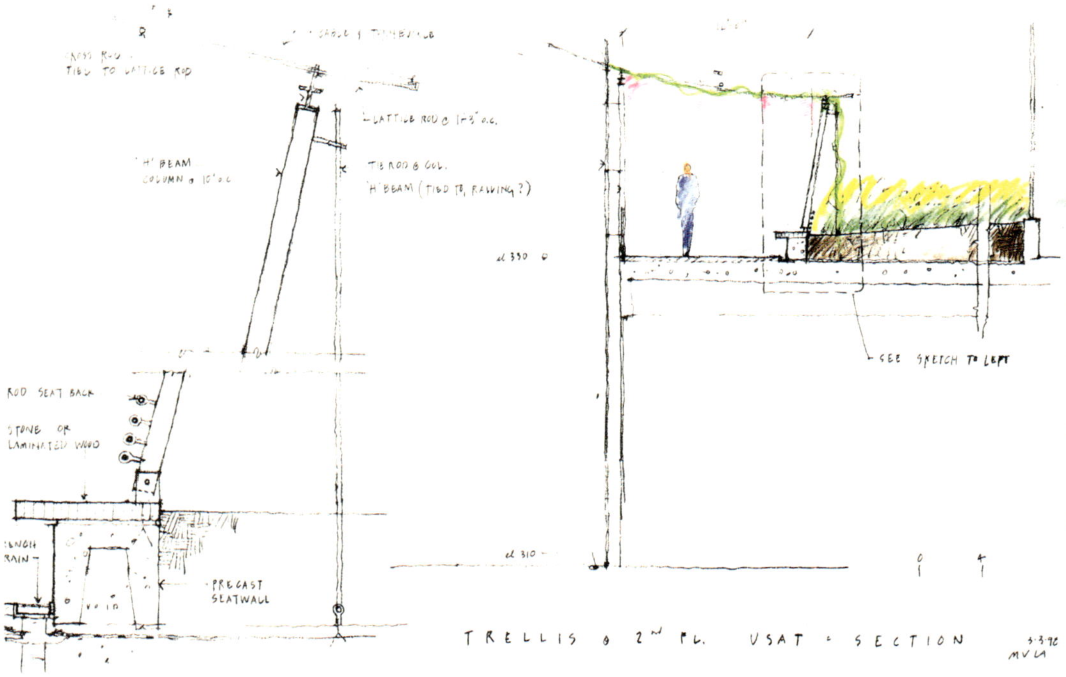

GRASSES
TREES
TREES
PERENNIALS
STEEL TRELLIS
AST WING
USA TODAY

Terrace Landscape Development — 4th Floor Terrace Section

**The focus of the two-story lobby is the dramatic stainless steel and granite harp stair.**

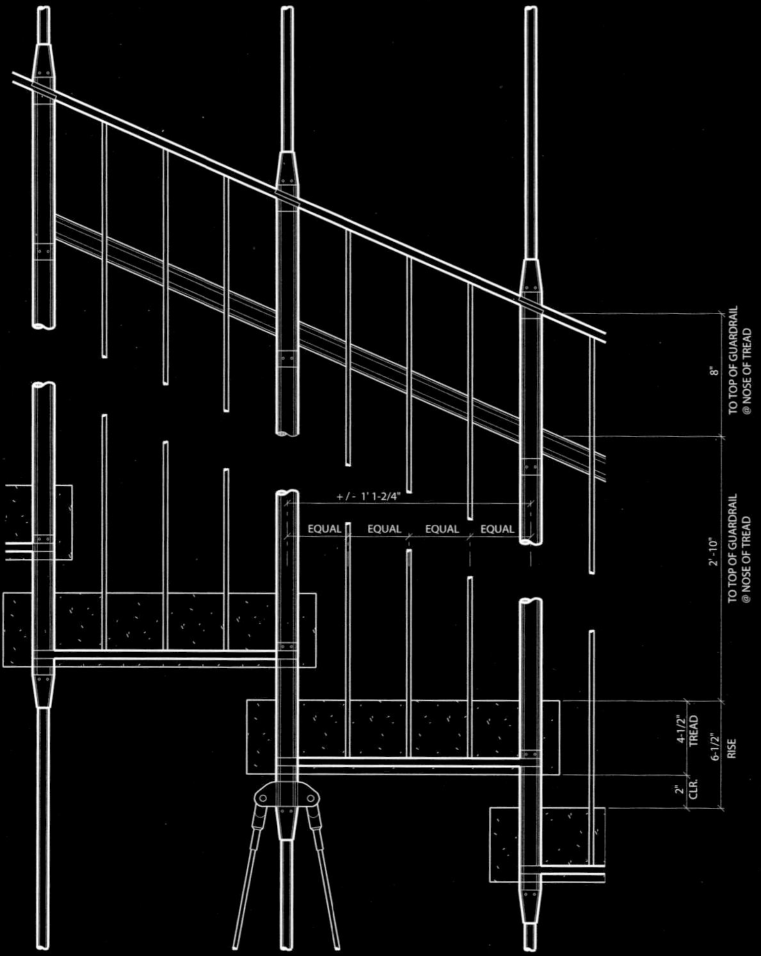

+ / - 1' 1-2/4"
EQUAL
EQUAL
EQUAL
EQUAL
8"
TO TOP OF GUARDRAIL
@ NOSE OF TREAD
2'-10"
TO TOP OF GUARDRAIL
@ NOSE OF TREAD
4-1/2"
TREAD
6-1/2"
RISE
2"
CLR.

5/8" DIA. ROD MIN.
(STAINLESS STEEL)
BAR
(STAINLESS STEEL)
HANDRAIL
(WOOD)
ROD
(STAINLESS STEEL)
1-1/4" DIA. PIPE (MIN.)
(STAINLESS STEEL)
TREAD
(STONE)
NOTE: TWO STRIPS
CASE-IN-PLACE ALUMINUM
OXIDE TREAD INSETS (TYP.)
SIX STRIPS @ LEADING TREAD
TREAD SUPPORT
(STAINLESS STEEL)

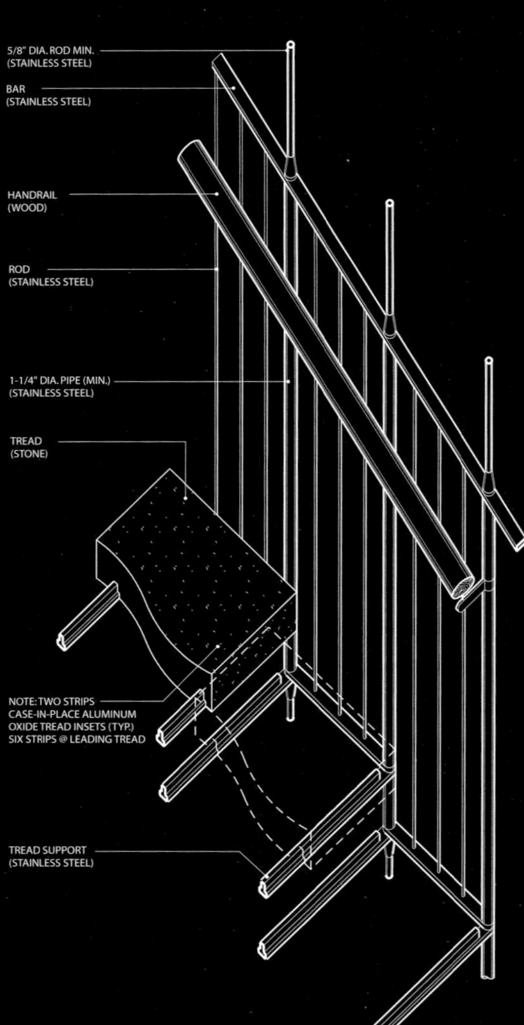

**Directly outside the harp stair is the lotus pool, blurring the distinction between inside and out.**

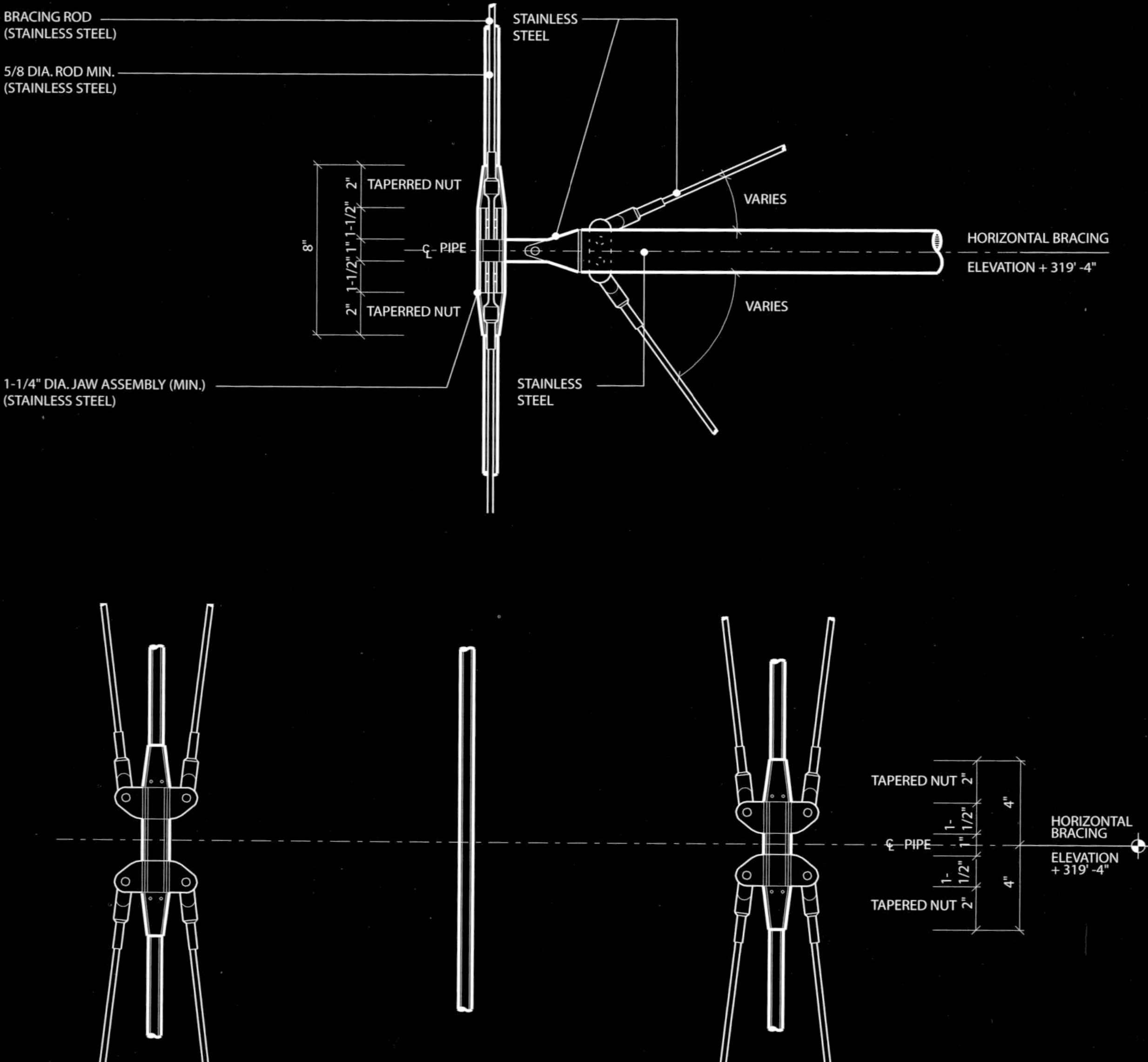

The harp staircase's polished Emerald Pearl granite steps
hang suspended from stainless steel rods.
The pool and landing are Absolute Black granite.

The exterior lotus pool is visually extended into the lobby via the pool beneath the stair.

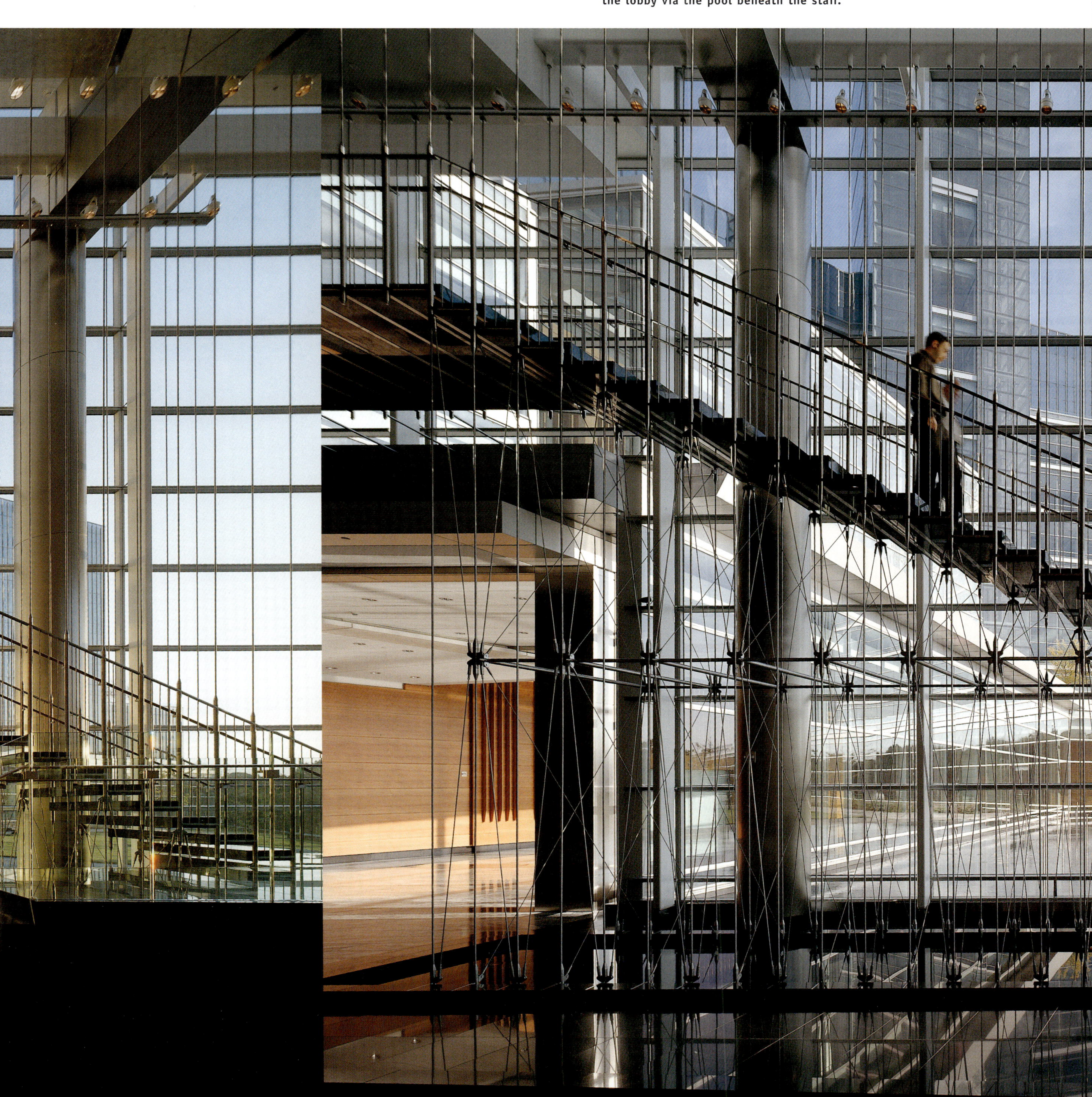

The use of clear low-e glass in the public spaces, such as the lobby and circulation corridors, helps reduce heating, cooling, and electricity loads.

The glass-wrapped lobby provides expansive views of, and access to, the courtyard.

The spectacular, cable-supported staircase hangs suspended from the skylight above.

The elevator tower, glowing from within, penetrates the lobby.

At the top of the stairs are the library and composing room for USA TODAY. A window into the composing room allows tours to look inside without disturbing work.

The White Cherokee marble floor reflects light up to the aluminum leaf ceiling.

William Pedersen's sketch of the completed design.

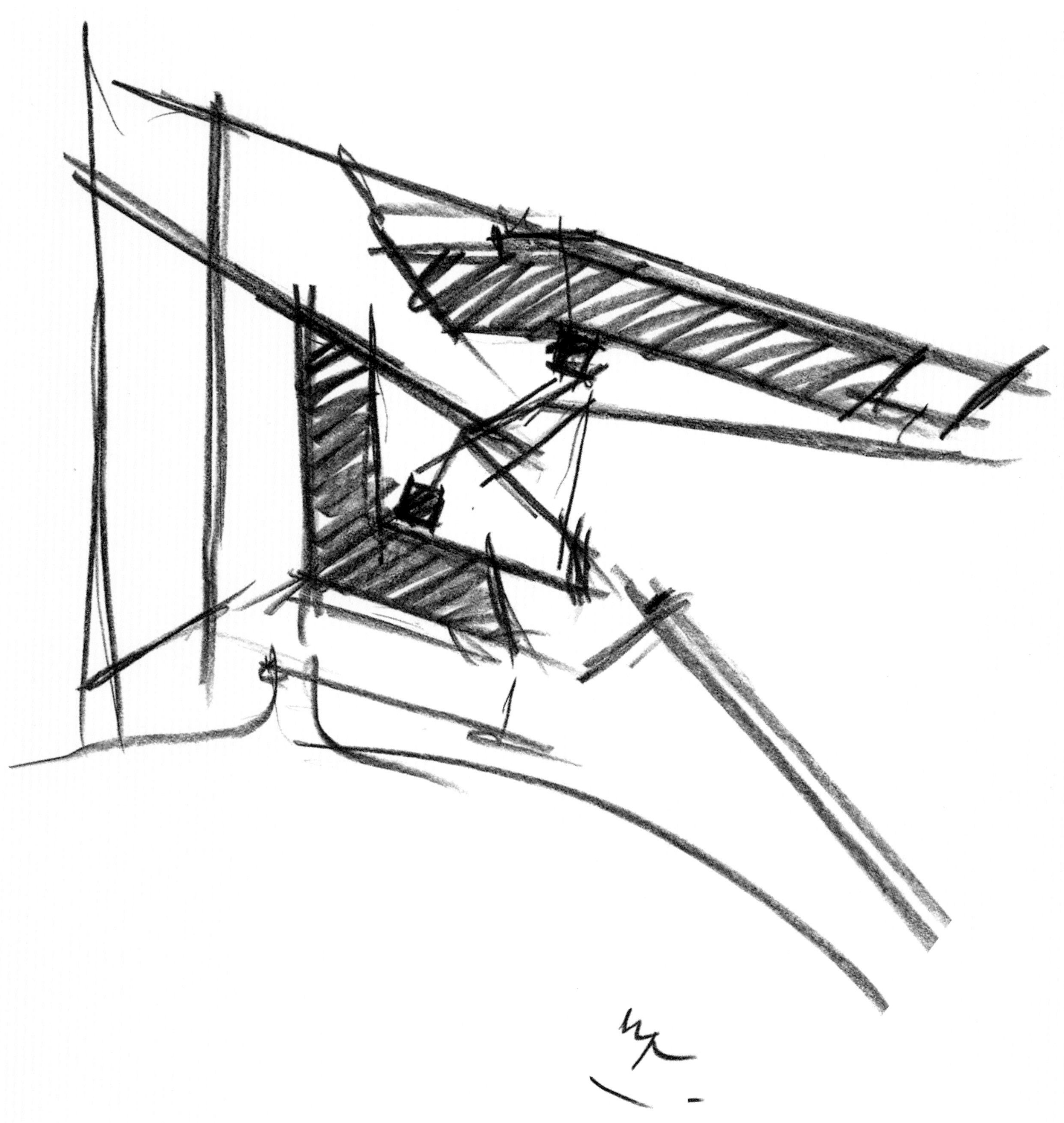

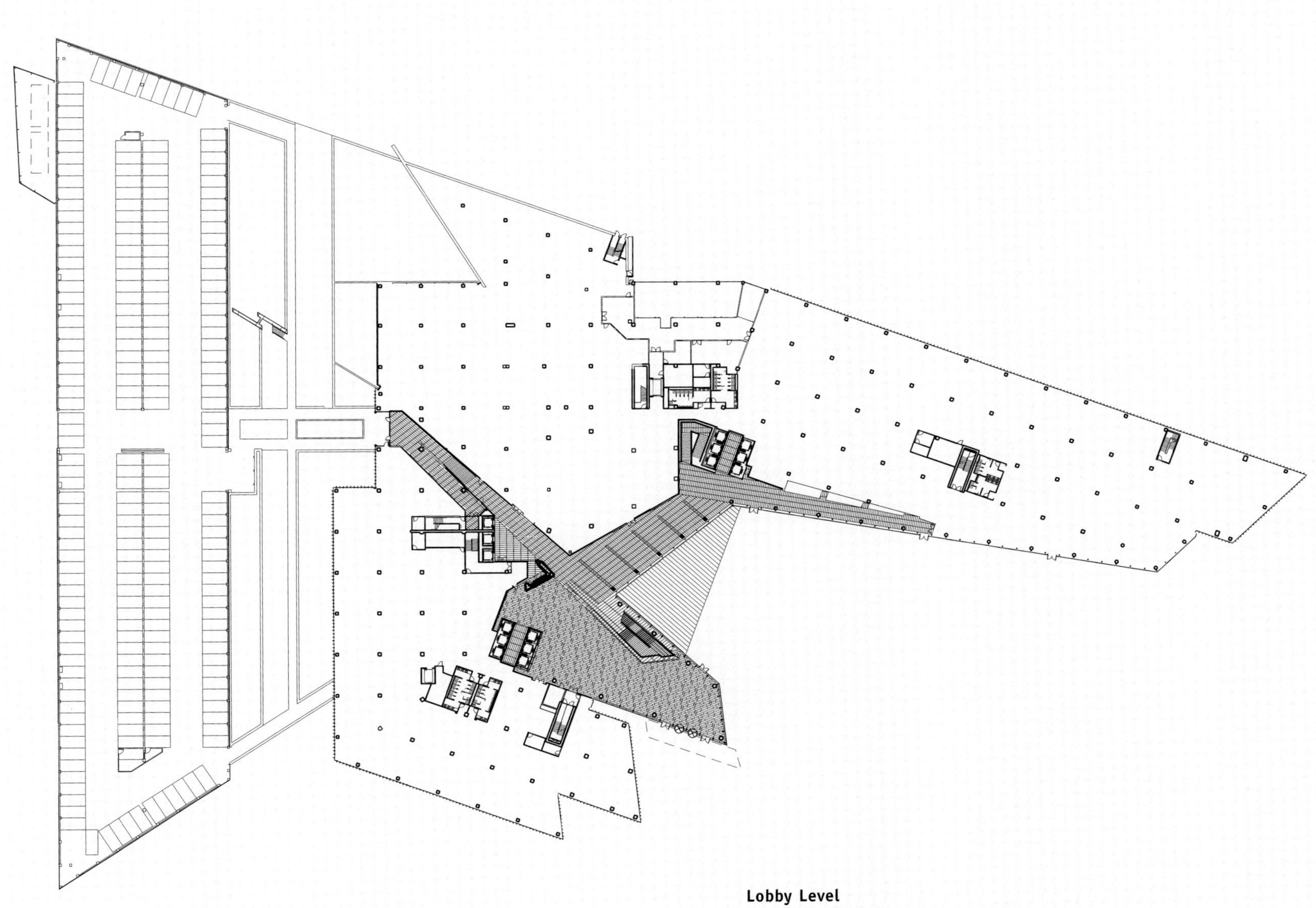

Lobby Level

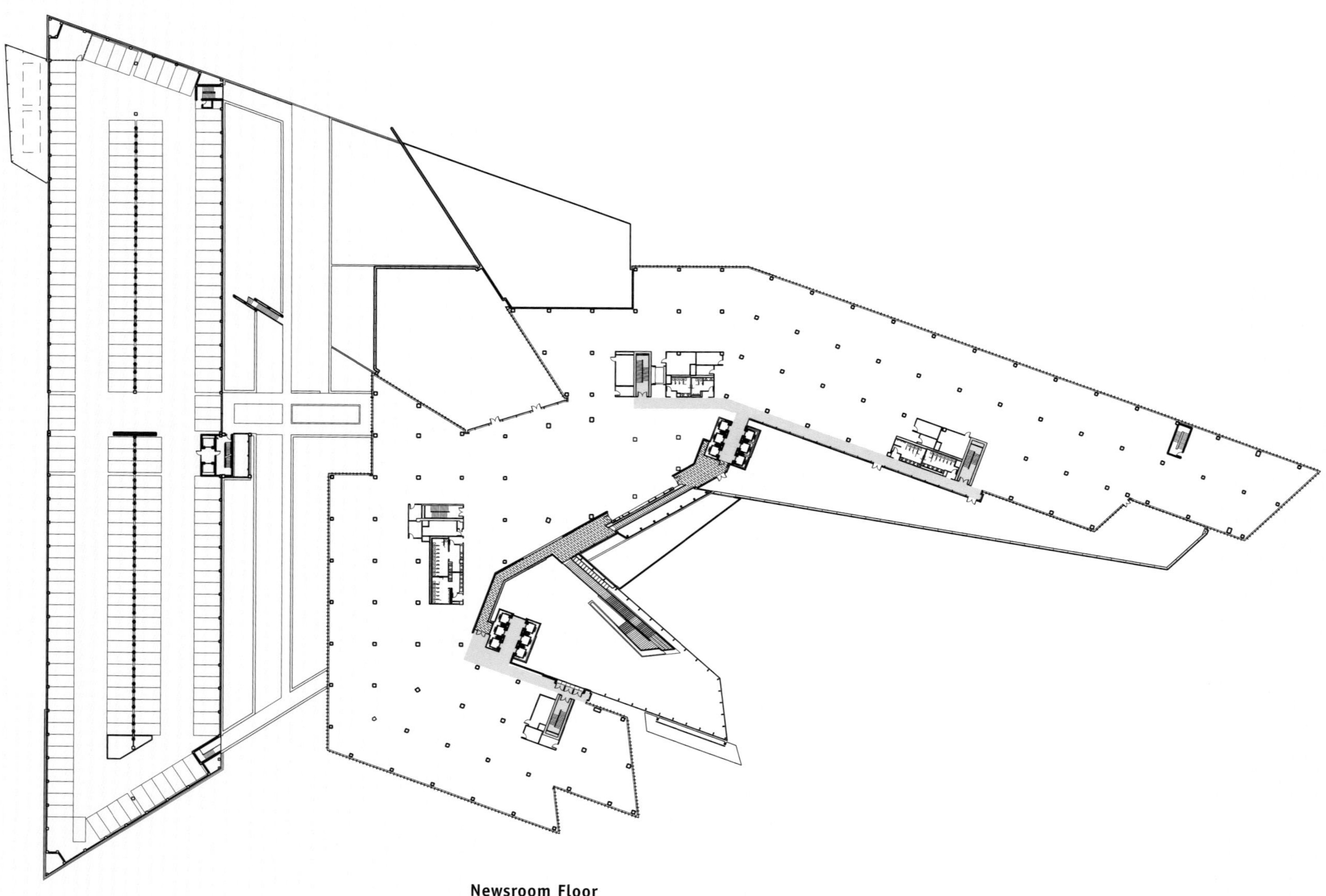

Newsroom Floor

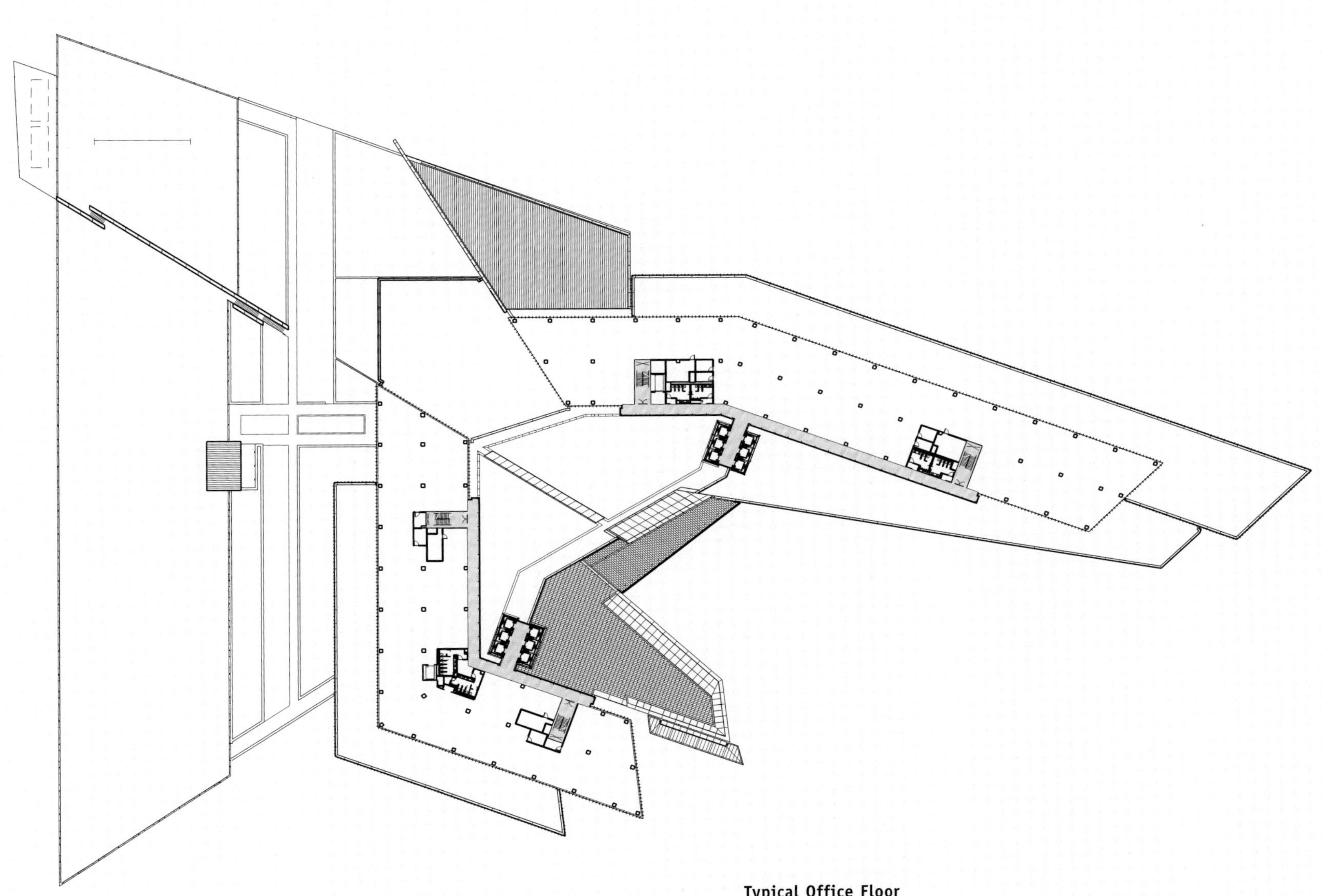

Typical Office Floor

The lobby has a very different feel in different light situations.
Opposite the stair's landing is the lobby desk
of acid-etched glass, stainless steel, and cherry wood.

View from the lobby toward the mezzanine level and terrace.

View from the mezzanine toward the lobby and harp staircase.

The bridge in the atrium connects the two towers.
In this space, the architects used low-e glass with a horizontal
ceramic frit pattern to reduce heat build-up and glare
while maintaining abundant light in the atrium.

View from below the atrium bridge. On the right is the three-story-high cherry wood wall that encloses the auditorium. The wood fins echo the glass fins on the building's exterior.

The enlarged billboard of Ed Ruscha's commissioned art piece is visible from this floor and the terrace level below via spatial slots in the floor.

Clear circulation corridors on the office floors face one another.
Mullions are minimized, while inset steel pipes brace against wind loads.

Beveled glass fins project rainbows of light.

Issues of light and materiality, transparency, translucency, reflectivity, and textural contrast are explored through material choice and the juxtaposition of the natural and the manmade, as is exemplified from within the transparent and translucent elevator towers.

The metal-clad stair slot leads up to the courts
and helipad on the parking garage roof.

Rusticated walls of local stone provide the base for the building volumes and extend into the landscape. Potomac basin stone from a local quarry in Maryland, used on most parkways in the region, is contextual while it reduces transport costs.

GANNETT
USA TODAY

Rising out of the landscape, the building is at once solid and effervescent in its lightness, reflectivity, and transparency. The glass fins create rainbow prisms of light that dance up the building's façades and through its corridors.

# Credits & Acknowledgements

**Gannett/USA Today Corporate Headquarters**
**McLean, Virginia**
**September 2001**

**Principal-In-Charge:**
A. Eugene Kohn

**Design Principal:**
William Pedersen

**Managing Principals:**
Robert L. Cioppa, Michael Greene

**Planning Principal:**
Jill Lerner

**Design Team Leaders:**
Jerri Smith, David Lukes

**Project Manager/Job Captains:**
Roger Robison, Takatomo Kashiwabara

**Project Team:**
Vlad Balla, Gertrudis Brens, Andrew Cleary, Jason Gomez,
Adolfo Guerrero, Miranti Gumayana, Eric Howeler,
Ming Leung, Nicholas Martone, Victor Pechaty, Audrey Torina,
Mark Townsend, Jason Wright

**Interior Architect:**
Lehman-Smith + McLeish

**Landscape:**
Michael Vergason Landscape Architects

**Curtain Wall Consultant:**
R.A. Heintges Architects

**Structural Engineer:**
CBM Engineers, Inc.

**Mechanical Engineer:**
TOLK, Inc.

**HVAC:**
TOLK, Inc.

**Electrical:**
TOLK, Inc.

**Lighting:**
Fisher Marantz Stone Partners

**Client/Owner:**
Gannett Company, Inc.

**Development Manager:**
Hines

**General Contractor:**
The Clark Construction Group

**Photography:**
Timothy Hursley, except:
Michael Dersin: p. 041, 083
Alex S. MacLean/Landslides: p. 018 (top)
Michael Vergason: p. 018 (bottom), 020

**Model Photography:**
Jock Pottle/Esto

Architecture has the power to positively transform the institutional culture of those it serves. It also has the power to strengthen the bonds of a community it encloses. Perhaps it is too early to tell if we have successfully fulfilled this potential for Gannett/USA TODAY. However, the early returns are positive.

We believe a building that promotes the concept of community should, itself, be created by a process which places a high value on a strategy of collaboration. For us, a successful collaborative process prizes the quality of an idea over its authorship. However, the quality of an architectural idea must also be tested and challenged by a diverse constituency to prove its merit. Client, developer, builder, and architect each must contribute to the dynamic of the design process. For over 25 years we have used this method to create architecture. Sometimes it works better than others. This time it worked exceptionally well and I want to acknowledge the participants, who made this building possible.

It has often been said, but it bears repeating, that a good building requires a good client. The leadership of Gannett/USA TODAY more than fulfilled this responsibility. Among several, we are particularly indebted to Tom Curley, President of USA TODAY, and to Nancy Houser, the owner's project manager, for their inspired leadership and constant support. A building like this does not come about without a unique dedication to quality. Before we ourselves were selected as architects, Gannett/USA TODAY asked the Gerald Hines group to assist them as development managers. Hines guided the process from architectural selection to the end of construction services and beyond. Their leadership was fundamental to the success of this project. We would like to thank Ken Hubbard, Bill Alsup, Greg Spivey, Lou Williams, and Patricia Reese for their contributions, their guidance, and their support.

For a building to fulfill its architectural potential it must be built with exceptional quality. Certainly, this is evident in every aspect of this structure. We are most grateful to the Clark Construction Company for accepting and rising to the challenge of this difficult design. This is not conventional construction; it is a finely crafted work created by the dedication of determined builders.

The large and complex consultant team responsible for the design and documentation of this building was assembled by the joint collaboration of Hines and Gannett/USA TODAY. Before we joined the team, Lehman-Smith + McLeish was asked to develop the program. Deborah Lehman-Smith led this most important phase of the work and subsequently led, with Jim McLeish, the design of the interior office spaces, the dining functions, and the auditorium. Their intimate knowledge of the owner's concerns and desires was invaluable in the process of balancing exterior constraints and internal function to determine the design direction. The support and confidence they brought made the final unconventional parti achievable. They also designed beautiful and functional interiors. We are very grateful to them.

The Hines organization brought the landscape architect Michael Vergason onto the team at the beginning of the design process. Their thoughtful site analysis and insightful comments on building orientation were contributions fundamental to the design direction. Ultimately, the exceptional linkage between building and landscape would not have been possible without their suggestions, talent and determination. Michael Vergason and Doug Hayes made possible a collaboration between our two disciplines which was most rewarding.

Within Kohn Pedersen Fox, several individuals must be acknowledged for their contributions. The strength of our collaboration and the pleasures of its dynamic will outlast, in my own mind, any accolades we receive for the actual product. This was, by any standard within my experience, an exceptionally positive adventure. We were determined to acknowledge the best ideas and were never hampered by the competition of individual egos. Gene Kohn, as always, provided invaluable advice and help whenever it was required. Robert Cioppa and Michael Greene masterfully guided the entire process through the inevitable difficulties that arise at all phases of the work. Roger Robison, with his extraordinary combination of tact and determination led the documentation and construction, supported by Takatomo Kashiwabara's tenacious dedication to precision. David Lukes, while still a young designer, contributed greatly to every aspect of this building's design with exceptional maturity and judgment. And finally, Jerri Smith, who, with me, has guided the design teams on so many of our best buildings, providing her unique blend of humor, selflessness, talent, and integrity.

William Pedersen
New York 2002